THE

ROMANCE

OF

TRISTAN

AND

ISEULT

AS RETOLD BY
JOSEPH BÉDIER
TRANSLATED BY
HILAIRE BELLOC
AND
COMPLETED BY
PAUL ROSENFELD

VINTAGE BOOKS
A DIVISION OF
RANDOM HOUSE
NEW YORK

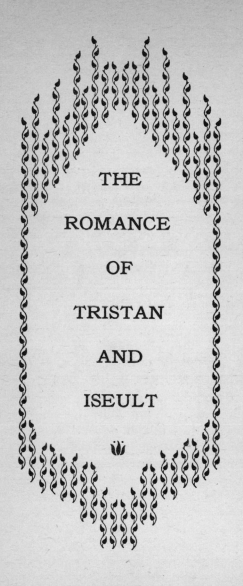

THE

ROMANCE

OF

TRISTAN

AND

ISEULT

PREFACE

In this book I have tried to avoid a mixture of the ancient and the modern. To steer clear of disparities, anachronisms and embellishments and, through the exercise of historical understanding and critical discipline, to avoid intrusion of our modern concepts into older forms of thinking and feeling, has been my aim, my effort, and no doubt, alas, my delusion. My text has been assembled from so many sources that, were I to enumerate them all in minute detail, this little volume would be weighed down by a profusion of footnotes. I owe, however, to the reader a general bibliographical outline.

Most of the fragments preserved of the ancient French poems have been published by Francisque Michel: *Tristan, receuil de ce qui reste des poèmes relatifs à ses aventures.* (Paris, Techener, 1835-1839.) Chapter I (The Childhood of Tristan) is a greatly abridged abstract from various poems, mainly from Thomas, the Anglo-Norman poet, as he appears in foreign adaptations. Chapters II and III are based on Eilhart von Oberg (Lichtenstein, Strassburg, 1878). Chapter IV (The Philtre) follows in its main lines tradition, but particularly Eilhart. Certain details are derived from Gottfried von Strassburg (W. Golther, Berlin and Stuttgart, 1888). Chapter V (Brangien) follows Eilhart. Chapter VI (The Tall Pine-Tree): Towards the middle of this chapter—when Iseult meets Tristan under the pine-tree—the story takes up the fragment of Béroul, which is followed faithfully in Chapters VII, VIII, IX, X, XI, with occasional interpretations according to Eilhart and various traditional sources. Chapter XII (The Ordeal by Iron): This is a very free summary of the anonymous fragment which follows the fragment of Béroul. Chapter XIII (The Voice of the Nightingale): Inserted according to a didactic poem of the 13th century, *Le Domnei des Amanz.* Chapter XIV (The Fairy Bell): Taken from Gottfried von Strassburg. Chapters XV-XVII: The episodes of Kariado and of Tristan as leper are taken from Thomas, the remaining text follows Eilhart. Chapter XVIII (Tristan Mad): Adaptation of a short French poem, which treats of the episode independently. Chapter XIX (Death): Translated from Thomas; certain episodes are taken from Eilhart, and from a French romance in prose, contained in manuscript 103 of the *Bibliothèque Nationale* in Paris.

JOSEPH BÉDIER

Chapters V, XIII, XVI and XVII, not included in the Hilaire Belloc translation, are translated by Paul Rosenfeld. Various passages in other chapters have also been inserted by Paul Rosenfeld, to make the English version correspond exactly to the French original in its definitive, enlarged edition.

CONTENTS

THE ROMANCE OF TRISTAN AND ISEULT

THE

CHILDHOOD

OF

TRISTAN

My lords, if you would hear a high tale of love and of death, here is that of Tristan and Queen Iseult; how to their full joy, but to their sorrow also, they loved each other, and how at last, they died of that love together upon one day; she by him and he by her.

Long ago, when Mark was King over Cornwall, Rivalen, King of Lyonesse, heard that Mark's enemies waged war on him; so he crossed the sea to bring him aid; and so faithfully did he serve him with counsel and sword that Mark gave him his sister Blanchefleur, whom King Rivalen loved most marvellously.

He wed her in Tintagel Minster, but hardly was she wed when the news came to him that his old enemy Duke Morgan had fallen on Lyonesse and was wasting town and field. Then Rivalen manned his ships in haste, and took Blanchefleur with him to his far land; but she was with child. He landed below his castle of Kanoël and gave the Queen in ward to his Marshal Rohalt, whom all men, because of his loyalty, called by a fair name, Rohalt the Keeper of Faith, and having summoned his barons set off to wage his war.

Blanchefleur waited for him continually, but he did not come home, till she learnt upon a day that Duke Morgan had killed him in foul ambush. She did not weep: she made no cry or lamentation, but her limbs failed her and grew weak, and her soul was filled with a strong desire to be rid of the flesh. Rohalt tried to soothe her:

"Queen," spoke he, "it is of no profit to pile grief on grief: those who are born, must they not also die? Pray God that he receive the dead and guard the living."

But she would not hear. Three days she awaited re-union with her lord, and on the fourth she brought forth a son; and taking him in her arms she said:

"Little son, I have longed a while to see you, and now I see you the fairest thing ever a woman bore. In sadness came I hither, in sadness did I bring forth, and in sadness has your first feast day gone. And as by sadness you came into the world, your name shall be called Tristan; that is the child of sadness."

After she had said these words she kissed him, and immediately when she had kissed him she died.

Rohalt, the Keeper of Faith, took the child, but already Duke Morgan's men besieged the Castle of Kanoël all round about. How was it possible for Rohalt to wage a long war? There is a wise saying: "Foolhardy was never hardy," and he was compelled to yield to Duke Morgan at his mercy: but for fear that Morgan might slay Rivalen's heir the Marshal hid him among his own sons.

When seven years were passed and the time had come to take the child from the women, Rohalt put Tristan under a good master, the squire Gorvenal, and Gorvenal taught him in a few years the arts that go with barony. He taught him the use of lance and sword and 'scutcheon and bow, and how to cast stone quoits and to leap wide dykes also: and he taught him to hate every lie and felony and to keep his given word; and he taught him the various kinds of song and harp-playing, and the hunter's craft; and when the child rode among the young squires you would have said that he and his horse and his armour were all one thing. To see him so noble and so proud, broad in the shoulders, lean of flank, loyal, strong and right, all men glorified Rohalt in such a son. But Rohalt remembering Rivalen and Blanchefleur (of whose youth and grace all this was a resurrection) loved him indeed as a son, but in his heart revered him as his lord.

Now all his joy was snatched from him on a day when certain merchants of Norway, having lured Tristan to their ship, bore him off as a rich prize, though Tristan fought hard, as a young wolf struggles, caught in a gin. But it is a truth well proved, and every sailor knows it, that the sea will hardly bear a felon ship, and gives no aid to rapine. The sea rose and cast a dark storm round the ship and drove it eight days and eight nights at random, till the mariners caught through the mist a coast of awful cliffs and sea-ward rocks whereon the sea would have ground their hull to pieces: then they did penance, knowing that the anger of the sea came of the lad, whom they had stolen in an evil hour, and they vowed his deliverance and got ready a boat to put him, if it might be, ashore: then the wind and sea fell and the sky shone, and as the Norway ship grew small in the offing, a quiet tide cast Tristan and the boat upon a beach of sand.

Painfully he climbed the cliff and saw, beyond, a lonely rolling heath and a forest stretching out and endless. And he wept, remembering Gorvenal, his father, and the land of Lyonesse. Then the distant cry of a hunt, with horse and hound came suddenly and lifted his heart, and a tall stag broke cover at the forest edge. The pack and the hunt streamed after it with a tumult of cries and winding horns, but just as the hounds were racing clustered at the haunch, the quarry turned to bay at a stone's throw from Tristan; a huntsman gave him the thrust, while all around the hunt had gathered and was winding the kill. But Tristan, seeing by the gesture of the huntsman that he made to cut the neck of the stag, cried out:

"My lord, what would you do? Is it fitting to cut up so noble a beast like any farm-yard hog? Is that the custom of this country?"

And the huntsman answered:

"Fair friend, what startles you? Why yes, first I take off the head of a stag, and then I cut it into four quarters and we carry it on our saddle bows to King

Mark, our lord: So do we, and so since the days of the first huntsmen have done the Cornish men. If, however, you know of some nobler custom, teach it us: take this knife and we will learn it willingly."

Then Tristan kneeled and skinned the stag before he cut it up, and quartered it all in order leaving the crow-bone all whole, as is meet, and putting aside at the end the head, the haunch, the tongue and the great heart's vein; and the huntsmen and the kennel hinds stood over him with delight, and the master huntsman said:

"Friend, these are good ways. In what land learnt you them? Tell us your country and your name."

"Good lord, my name is Tristan, and I learnt these ways in my country of Lyonesse."

"Tristan," said the master huntsman, "God reward the father that brought you up so nobly; doubtless he is a baron, rich and strong."

Now Tristan knew both speech and silence, and he answered:

"No lord; my father is a burgess. I left his home unbeknownst upon a ship that trafficked to a far place, for I wished to learn how men lived in foreign lands. But if you will accept me of the hunt I will follow you gladly and teach you other crafts of venery."

"Fair Tristan, I marvel there should be a land where a burgess's son can know what a knight's son knows not elsewhere, but come with us since you will it; and welcome: we will bring you to King Mark, our lord."

Tristan completed his task; to the dogs he gave the heart, the head, offal and ears; and he taught the hunt how the skinning and the ordering should be done. Then he thrust the pieces upon pikes and gave them to this huntsman and to that to carry, to one the snout to another the haunch to another the flank to another the chine; and he taught them how to ride by twos in rank, according to the dignity of the pieces each might bear.

So they took the road and spoke together, till they came on a great castle and round it fields and orchards, and living waters and fish ponds and plough lands, and many ships were in its haven, for that castle stood above the sea. It was well fenced against all assault or engines of war, and its keep, which the giants had built long ago, was compact of great stones, like a chess board of vert and azure.

And when Tristan asked its name:

"Good liege," they said, "we call it Tintagel."

And Tristan cried:

"Tintagel! Blessed be thou of God, and blessed be they that dwell within thee."

(Therein, my lords, therein had Rivalen taken Blanchefleur to wife, though their son knew it not.)

When they came before the keep the horns brought the barons to the gates and King Mark himself. And when the master huntsman had told him all the story, and King Mark had marvelled at the good order of the cavalcade, and the cutting of the stag, and the high art of venery in all, yet most he wondered at the stranger boy, and still gazed at him, troubled and wondering whence came his tenderness, and his heart would answer him nothing; but, my lords, it was blood that spoke, and the love he had long since borne his sister Blanchefleur.

That evening, when the boards were cleared, a singer out of Wales, a master, came forward among the barons in hall and sang a harper's song, and as this harper touched the strings of his harp, Tristan who sat at the King's feet, spoke thus to him:

"Oh master, that is the first of songs! The Bretons of old wove it once to chant the loves of Graëlent. And the melody is rare and rare are the words: master, your voice is subtle: harp us that well."

But when the Welshman had sung, he answered:

"Boy, what do you know of the craft of music? If the burgesses of Lyonesse teach their sons harp-play also, and rotes and viols too, rise, and take this harp and show your skill."

Then Tristan took the harp and sang so well that the barons softened as they heard, and King Mark marvelled at the harper from Lyonesse whither so long ago Rivalen had taken Blanchefleur away.

When the song ended, the King was silent a long space, but he said at last:

"Son, blessed be the master that taught thee, and blessed be thou of God: for God loves good singers. Their voices and the voice of the harp enter the souls of men and wake dear memories and cause them to forget many a mourning and many a sin. For our joy did you come to this roof, stay near us a long time, friend."

And Tristan answered:

"Very willingly will I serve you, Sire, as your harper, your huntsman and your liege."

So did he, and for three years a mutual love grew up in their hearts. By day Tristan followed King Mark at pleas and in saddle; by night he slept in the royal room with the councillors and the peers, and if the King was sad he would harp to him to soothe his care. The barons also cherished him, and (as you shall learn) Dinas of Lidan, the seneschal, beyond all others. And more tenderly than the barons and than Dinas the King loved him. But Tristan could not forget, or Rohalt his father, or his master Gorvenal, or the land of Lyonesse.

My lords, a teller that would please, should not stretch his tale too long, and truly this tale is so various and so high that it needs no straining. Then let me shortly tell how Rohalt himself, after long wandering by sea and land, came into Cornwall, and found Tristan, and showing the King the carbuncle that once was Blanchefleur's, said:

"King Mark, here is your nephew Tristan, son of your sister Blanchefleur and of King Rivalen. Duke Morgan holds his land most wrongfully; it is time such land came back to its lord."

And Tristan (in a word) when his uncle had armed him knight, crossed the sea, and was hailed of his father's vassals, and killed Rivalen's slayer and was re-seized of his land.

Then remembering how King Mark could no longer live in joy without him, and as the nobility of his heart ever revealed the wisest course to him, he summoned his council and his barons and said this:

"Lords of the Lyonesse, I have retaken this place and I have avenged King Rivalen by the help of God and of you. Thus I have rendered to my father what is due him. But two men Rohalt and King Mark of Cornwall nourished me, an orphan, and a wandering boy. So should I call them also fathers. To those, too, must I not also render what is their due? Now a free man has two things thoroughly his own, his body and his land. To Rohalt then, here, I will release my land. Do you hold it, father, and your son shall hold it after you. But my body I give up to King Mark. I will leave this country, dear though it be, and in Cornwall I will serve King Mark as my lord. Such is my judgment, but you, my lords of Lyonesse, are my lieges, and owe me counsel; if then, some one of you will counsel me another thing let him rise and speak."

But all the barons praised him, though they wept; and taking with him Gorvenal only, Tristan set sail for King Mark's land.

THE

MORHOLT

OUT

OF

IRELAND

When Tristan came back to that land, King Mark and all his Barony were mourning; for the King of Ireland had manned a fleet to ravage Cornwall, should King Mark refuse, as he had refused these fifteen years, to pay a tribute his fathers had paid.

For know you, certain old treaties gave the men of Ireland the right to levy on the men of Cornwall one year three hundred pounds of copper, another year three hundred pounds of silver, a third year three hundred pounds of gold. When came the fourth year they might take with them three hundred youths and three hundred maidens, of fifteen years of age, drawn by lot among the Cornish folk.

Now that year this King had sent to Tintagel, to carry his summons, a giant knight; the Morholt, whose sister he had wed, and whom no man had yet been able to overcome: so King Mark had summoned all the barons of his land to Council, by letters sealed.

On the day assigned, when the barons were gathered in hall, and when the King had taken his throne, the Morholt said these things:

"King Mark, hear for the last time the summons of the King of Ireland, my lord. He arraigns you to pay at last that which you have owed so long, and because you have refused it too long already he bids you give over to me this day three hundred youths and three hundred maidens drawn by lot from among the Cornish folk. My ship, anchored in the port of Tintagel, will bear them away that they may become our serfs. Nevertheless—and I except only yourself, King Mark, as is meet—if it so be that any one of your barons would prove by trial of combat that the King of Ireland receives this tribute without right, I will take up his wager. Which among you, my Cornish lords, will fight to redeem this land?"

The barons glanced at each other but all were silent. This one said to himself: "Unhappy man, behold the stature of the Morholt of Ireland: he is stronger than four robust men. Behold his sword: know you not that by magic it has struck off the heads of the bravest champions in all the years since the King of Ireland has sent this giant to carry his challenges among the vassal lands? Weakling, do you court death? To what end would you tempt God?" That one thought: "Is it to become serfs that I have reared you, my dear sons, and you, my dear daughters, to become harlots? But my death would not save you."

And all were silent.

Again the Morholt spoke:

"Lords of Cornwall, which among you accepts my challenge? I offer him a noble battle. Three days hence we will go by boats to the islet of St. Samson's in the offing of Tintagel. There your champion and I will fight in single combat, and the glory of the battle will honour all his kin."

Still they were silent, and the Morholt resembled an hawk shut in a cage with small birds: when he enters, all grow mute.

For the third time the Morholt spoke:

"Very well, rare Cornish lords, since this course seems the nobler to you: draw your children by lot that I may bear them away. But I did not believe this land was inhabited only by serfs."

Then Tristan knelt at the feet of King Mark and said:

"Lord King, by your leave I will do battle."

And in vain would King Mark have turned him from his purpose, thinking, how could even valour save so young a knight? But he threw down his gage to the Morholt, and the Morholt took up the gage.

On the appointed day he had himself clad for a great feat of arms in a hauberk and in a steel helm. The barons wept for pity of the valiant knight and for shame of themselves. "Ah, Tristan," said they to themselves, "fearless baron, fair youth, why have not I rathermore than you, undertaken this battle? My death would bring less sorrow to this earth!"— The bells pealed, and all, those of the nobility and those of low degree, old men, children and women, weeping and praying, escorted Tristan to the shore. They still had hope, for hope in the heart of men lives on lean pasture.

Tristan entered a boat and drew to the islet of St. Samson's, where the knights were to fight each to each alone. Now the Morholt had hoisted to his mast a sail of rich purple, and coming fast to land, he moored his boat on the shore. But Tristan pushed off his own boat adrift with his feet.

"Vassal, what is it you do?" said the Morholt, "and why have you not fastened your boat with a mooring-line as I have done?"

"Vassal, why should I?" Tristan answered. "One of us only will go hence alive. One boat will serve."

And each rousing the other to the fray they passed into the isle.

No man saw the sharp combat; but thrice the salt sea-breeze had wafted or seemed to waft a cry of fury to the land. Then in sign of mourning the women beat their palms in chorus, and massed to one side before their tent, the companions of the Morholt laughed.

Then at last towards the hour of noon the purple sail showed far off; the Irish boat appeared from the island shore, and there rose a clamour of distress: "The Morholt! The Morholt!" When suddenly, as the boat grew larger on the sight and topped a wave, they saw that a knight stood at its prow. Each of his hands brandished a sword: it was Tristan. Immediately twenty boats launched forth and the young men swam out to meet him. The good knight leapt ashore, and as the mothers kissed the steel upon his feet he cried to the Morholt's men:

"My lords of Ireland, the Morholt fought well. See here, my sword is broken and a splinter of it stands fast in his head. Take you that steel, my lords: it is the tribute of Cornwall."

Then he went up to Tintagel and as he went the people he had freed waved green boughs, and rich cloths were hung at the windows. But when Tristan reached the castle amid a jubilation, a pealing of bells, a sounding of horns and trumpets so lusty that one could not have heard God had He thundered, he drooped in the arms of King Mark, for the blood ran from his wounds.

The Morholt's men, they landed in Ireland quite cast down. For when ever he came back into White-haven the Morholt had been wont to take joy in the sight of his clan upon the shore, of the Queen his sister, and of his niece Iseult the Fair, the golden-haired, whose beauty already shone like the breaking dawn. Tenderly had they cherished him of old, and had he taken some wound, they healed him, for they were skilled in balms and potions. But now their magic was vain, for he lay dead, sewn in a deer hide, and the splinter of the foreign brand yet stood in his skull till Iseult plucked it out and shut it in an ivory coffer, precious as a reliquary. And, bowed over the tall corpse, mother and daughter ceaselessly repeated the praises of the dead man, ceaselessly hurled an imprecation at the murderer, and by turns led the women in the funeral dirge.

From that day Iseult the Fair knew and hated the name of Tristan of Lyonesse.

But over in Tintagel Tristan languished, for there trickled a poisonous blood from his wound. The doctors found that the Morholt had thrust into him a poisoned barb and as their potions and their theriac could never heal him they left him in God's hands. So hateful a stench came from his wound that all his dearest friends fled him, all save King Mark, Gorvenal and Dinas of Lidan. They always could stay near his couch because their love overcame their abhorrence. At last Tristan had himself carried into a hut apart on the shore; and lying facing the sea he awaited death. He thought: "Have you thus abandoned me, King Mark, me who saved the honour of your land? No, I know, fair uncle, that you would give your life for mine: but what avails your tenderness? I must die. Yet it is good to see the sun and my heart is still high. I would like to try the sea that brings all chances. . . . I would have the sea bear me far off alone, to what land no matter, so that it heal me of my wound. And perchance some day I will once more serve you, fair uncle, as your harper, your huntsman and your liege."

He begged so long that King Mark accepted his desire. He bore him into a boat with neither sail nor oar, and Tristan wished that his harp only should be placed beside him: for sails he could not lift, nor oar ply, nor sword wield; and as a seaman on some long voyage casts to the sea a beloved companion dead, so Gorvenal pushed out to sea that boat where his dear son lay; and the sea drew him away.

For seven days and seven nights the sea so drew him; at times to charm his grief, he harped; and when at last the sea brought him near a shore where fishermen had left their port that night to fish far out, they heard as they rowed a sweet and strong and living tune that ran above the sea, and feathering their oars they listened immovable.

In the first whiteness of the dawn they saw the boat at large. "Thus," said they to themselves, "did supernatural music surround St. Brandan's ship while it sailed to the Fortunate Isles over a sea as white as milk." They rowed towards the boat. She went at random and nothing seemed to live in her except the voice of the harp. But as they neared, the air grew weaker and died; and when they hailed her Tristan's hands had fallen lifeless on the strings though they still trembled. The fishermen took him in and bore him back to port, to their lady who was merciful and perhaps would heal him.

It was that same port of Whitehaven where the Morholt lay, and their lady was Iseult the Fair.

She alone, being skilled in philtres could save Tristan, but she alone wished him dead. When Tristan knew himself again (for her art restored him) he knew himself to be in a land of peril. But he was yet strong to hold his own and found good crafty words. He told a tale of how he was a seer that had taken passage on a merchant ship and sailed to Spain to learn the art of reading all the stars—of how pirates had boarded the ship and of how, though wounded, he had fled into that boat. He was believed, nor did any of the Morholt's men know his face again, so hardly had the poison used it. But when, after forty days, Iseult of the Golden Hair had all but healed him, when already his limbs had recovered and the grace of youth returned, he knew that he must escape, and he fled and after many dangers he came again before Mark the King.

THE
QUEST
OF
THE
LADY
WITH
THE
HAIR
OF
GOLD

My lords, there were in the court of King Mark four barons, the basest of men, who hated Tristan with a hard hate, for his greatness and for the tender love the King bore him. And well I know their names: Andret, Guenelon, Gondoïne and Denoalen. Like Tristan, Andret was a nephew of King Mark's. They knew that the King had intent to grow old childless and to leave his land to Tristan; and their envy swelled and by lies they angered the chief men of Cornwall against Tristan. They said:

"There have been too many marvels in this man's

life: but you are men of wit, my lords, and without doubt you can explain them. It was marvel enough that he beat the Morholt, but by what sorcery did he try the sea alone at the point of death, or which of us, my lords, could voyage without mast or sail? They say that warlocks can. It was sure a warlock feat, and that is a warlock harp of his pours poison daily into the King's heart. See how he has bent that heart by power and chain of sorcery! He will be king yet, my lords, and you will hold your lands of a wizard."

They brought over the greater part of the barons, for most men are unaware that what is in the power of magicians to accomplish, that the heart also can accomplish by dint of love and bravery. These barons pressed King Mark to take to wife some king's daughter who should give him an heir, or else they threatened to return each man into his keep and wage him war. But the King turned against them and swore in his heart that so long as his dear nephew lived no king's daughter should come to his bed. Then in his turn did Tristan (in his shame to be thought to serve for hire) threaten that if the King did not yield to his barons, he would himself go over sea and serve some great king. At this, King Mark made a term with his barons and gave them forty days to hear his decision.

On the appointed day he waited alone in his chamber and sadly mused: "Where shall I find a king's daughter so fair and yet so distant that I may feign to wish her my wife?"

Just then by his window that looked upon the sea two building swallows came in quarrelling together. Then, startled, they flew out, but had let fall from their beaks a woman's hair, long and fine, and shining like a beam of light.

King Mark took it, and called his barons and Tristan and said:

"To please you, lords, I will take a wife; but you must seek her whom I have chosen."

"Fair lord, we wish it all," they said, "and who may she be?"

"Why," said he, "she whose hair this is; nor will I take another."

"And whence, lord King, comes this hair of gold; who brought it and from what land?"

"It comes, my lords, from the lady with the hair of gold, the swallows brought it me. They know from what country it came."

Then the barons saw themselves mocked and cheated, and they turned with sneers to Tristan, for they thought him to have counselled the trick. But Tristan, when he had looked on the hair of gold, remembered Iseult the Fair and smiled and said this:

"King Mark, can you not see that the doubts of these lords shame me? You have designed in vain. I will go seek the lady with the hair of gold. The search is perilous and it will be more difficult for me to return from her land than from the isle where I slew the Morholt; nevertheless, my uncle, I would once more put my body and my life into peril for you; and that your barons may know I love you loyally, I take this oath, to die on the adventure or to bring back to this castle of Tintagel the queen with that fair hair."

He fitted out a great ship and loaded it with corn and wine, with honey and all manner of good things; he manned it with Gorvenal and a hundred young knights of high birth, chosen among the bravest, and he clothed them in coats of home-spun and in hair cloth so that they seemed merchants only: but under the deck he hid rich cloth of gold and scarlet as for a great king's messengers.

When the ship had taken the sea the helmsman asked him:

"Lord, to what land shall I steer?"

"Sir," said he, "steer for Ireland, straight for Whitehaven harbour."

The helmsman trembled. Did not Tristan know that, since the murder of Morholt, the King of Ireland harried all Cornish ships, and seizing their sailors, hung them at the crossroads? Nevertheless the helmsman obeyed and reached the dangerous land.

At first Tristan made believe to the men of Whitehaven that his friends were merchants of England come peacefully to barter; but as these strange merchants passed the day in the useless games of draughts and chess, and seemed to know dice better than the bargain-price of corn, Tristan feared discovery and knew not how to pursue his quest.

Now it chanced once upon the break of day that he heard a cry so terrible that one would have called it a demon's cry; nor had he ever heard a brute bellow in such wise, so awful and strange it seemed. He called a woman who passed by the harbour, and said:

"Tell me, lady, whence comes that voice I have heard, and hide me nothing."

"My lord," said she, "I will tell you truly. It is the roar of a dragon the most terrible and dauntless upon earth. Daily it leaves its den and stands at one of the gates of the city: Nor can any come out or go in till a maiden has been given up to it; and when it has her in its claws it devours her in less time than it takes to say a Pater Noster."

"Lady," said Tristan, "make no mock of me, but tell me straight: Can a man born of woman kill this thing?"

"Fair sir, and gentle," she said, "I cannot say; but this is sure: Twenty knights and tried have run the venture, because the King of Ireland has published it that he will give his daughter, Iseult the Fair, to whomsoever shall kill the beast; but it has devoured them all."

Tristan left the woman and returning to his ship armed himself in secret, and it was a fine sight to see so noble a charger and so good a knight come out from such a merchant-hull: but the haven was empty of folk, for the dawn had barely broken and none saw him as he rode to the gate. And hardly had he passed it, when he met suddenly five men at full gallop flying towards the town. Tristan seized one by his red braided hair, as he passed, and dragged him over his mount's crupper and held him fast:

"God save you, my lord," said he, "and whence does the dragon come?" And when the other had shewn him by what road, he let him go.

As the monster neared, he showed the head of a bear and red eyes like coals of fire and hairy tufted ears; lion's claws, a serpent's tail, and a griffin's body.

Tristan charged his horse at him so strongly that, though the beast's mane stood with fright yet he drove at the dragon: his lance struck its scales and shivered. Then Tristan drew his sword and struck at the dragon's head, but he did not so much as cut the hide. The beast felt the blow: with its claws he dragged at the shield and broke it from the arm; then, his breast unshielded, Tristan used the sword again and struck so strongly that the air rang all round about: but in vain, for he could not wound and meanwhile the dragon vomited from his nostrils two streams of loathsome flames, and Tristan's helm blackened like a cinder and his horse stumbled and fell down and died; but Tristan standing on his feet thrust his sword right into the beast's jaws, and split its heart in two. The dragon uttered his hideous scream a last time and died.

Then he cut out the tongue and put it into his hose, but as the poison came against his flesh the hero fainted and fell in the high grass that bordered the marsh around.

Now the man with the braided red hair whom he had stopped in flight was Aguynguerran the Red, the seneschal of Ireland, and he desired Iseult the Fair; and though he was a coward, yet such is the power of love that every morning he placed himself in ambush, fully armed, in order to attack the monster. But when he heard its cry even at a distance the good knight fled. That day he had dared so far as to return with his companions secretly, and as he found the dragon vanquished, the horse dead, the shield broken, he thought that the victor had died in some lonely spot. So he cut off the monster's head and bore it to the King, and claimed the great reward.

The King could credit his prowess but hardly, yet wished justice done and summoned his vassals to court, so that there, before the barony assembled, the seneschal should furnish proof of his victory won.

When Iseult the Fair heard that she was to be given to this coward first she laughed long, and then she wailed. But on the morrow, doubting some trick, she took with her Perinis her squire and Brangien her maid, and all three rode unbeknownst towards the dragon's lair: and Iseult saw such a trail on the road as made her wonder—for the hoofs that made it had never been shod in her land. Then she came on the dragon, headless, and a dead horse beside him: nor was the horse harnessed in the fashion of Ireland. Some foreign man had slain the beast, but they knew not whether he still lived or not.

They sought him long, Iseult and Perinis and Brangien together, till at last Brangien saw the helm glittering in the marshy grass: and Tristan still breathed. Perinis put him on his horse and bore him secretly to the women's rooms. There Iseult told her mother the tale and left the hero with her, and as the Queen unharnessed him, the dragon's tongue fell from his boot of steel. Then, the Queen of Ireland revived him by the virtue of an herb and said:

"Stranger, I know you for the true slayer of the dragon: but our seneschal, a felon, cut off its head and claims my daughter Iseult for his wage; will you be ready two days hence to give him the lie in battle?"

"Queen," said he, "the time is short, but you, I think, can cure me in two days. Upon the dragon I conquered Iseult, and on the seneschal perhaps I shall reconquer her."

Then the Queen brewed him strong brews, and on the morrow Iseult the Fair got him ready a bath and anointed him with a balm her mother had conjured. Her glance lingered on the face of the wounded man; she saw that he was beautiful and thought to herself: "Truly, if his prowess equals his beauty, my champion will fight a brave battle." Restored by the warmth of the water and the vigour of the spices,

Tristan looked at her, and as he looked at her he thought: "So I have found the Queen of the Hair of Gold," and he smiled as he thought it. But Iseult, noting it, thought: "Why did this stranger smile? Have I done something unsuitable? Have I omitted one of the services which a maiden owes a guest? Perhaps he smiled because he thinks I forgot to burnish his armour which the poison tarnished?"

She went to were Tristan's armour lay. "This helmet is of good steel," thought she, "and will not fail in the hour of need. And this coat of mail is strong, light, worthy to be worn by a brave knight." She took the sword by the hilt: "Truly, this is a fine blade, and one which fits a daring baron." To wipe it clean, she drew the blood-stained sword from its rich sheath. She saw that it was heavily notched; noticed the shape of the dent: was not this the blade that had broken off in Morholt's skull? She balanced a moment in doubt, then she went to where she kept the steel she had found in the skull and she put it to the sword, and it fitted so that the join was hardly seen.

She ran to where Tristan lay wounded, and with the sword above him she cried:

"You are that Tristan of the Lyonesse, who killed the Morholt, my mother's brother, and now you shall die in your turn."

Tristan strained to ward the blow, but he was too weak; his wit, however, stood firm in spite of evil and he said:

"So be it, let me die: but to save yourself long memories, listen awhile: King's daughter, my life is not only in your power but is yours of right. My life is yours because you have twice returned it me. Once, long ago: for I was the wounded harper whom you healed of the poison of the Morholt's shaft. Nor repent the healing: were not these wounds had in fair fight? Did I kill the Morholt by treason? Had he not defied me and was I not held to the defence of my body? And now this second time also you have saved me. It was for you I fought the beast. . . .

"But let us leave these things. I would but show you how my life is your own. Kill me then, if you think thus to win praise and glory. Doubtless, when you are lying in the arms of the brave seneschal, it will be sweet for you to think of your wounded guest, who wagered his life to conquer you, and did conquer you, and whom you slew defenceless in this bath."

Iseult replied: "I hear strange words. Why should he that killed the Morholt seek me also, his niece? Doubtless because the Morholt came for a tribute of maidens from Cornwall, so you came to boast returning that you had brought back the maiden who was nearest to him, to Cornwall, a slave."

"King's daughter," said Tristan, "no. . . . One day two swallows flew, and flew to Tintagel and bore one hair out of all your hairs of gold, and I thought they brought me good will and peace, so I came to find you over seas. So I braved the monster and his poison. See here, amid the threads of gold upon my coat your hair is sown: the threads are tarnished, but your bright hair still shines."

Iseult put down the sword and taking up the coat of arms she saw upon it the hair of gold and was silent a long space, till she kissed him on the lips to prove peace, and she put rich garments over him.

On the day of the barons' assembly, Tristan sent

Perinis privily to his ship to summon his companions that they should come to court adorned as befitted the envoys of a great king, for it was his hope that very day to reach the goal of his adventure. Gorvenal and the hundred knights had grieved for four days now, thinking Tristan lost. The tidings delighted them.

One by one the hundred knights passed into the hall where all the barons of Ireland stood, they entered in silence and sat all in rank together: on their scarlet and purple the gems gleamed.

The Irishmen spake among themselves: "Whoever are these splendid lords? Who knows them? Behold these sumptuous cloaks trimmed with sable and with embroideries. Behold the shimmer, at the hilts of their swords, the buckles of their garments, of rubies, beryls, emeralds and many stones of very names we do not know. Who ever has seen splendour equal to this? Whence come these lords? Whose are they?" But the hundred knights said nothing and did not move from their seats, no matter who entered.

When the King had taken his throne, the seneschal arose to prove by witness and by arms that he had slain the dragon and that so Iseult was won. Then Iseult bowed to her father and said:

"King, I have here a man who challenges your seneschal for lies and felony. Promise that you will pardon this man all his past deeds, no matter what they were, for here he stands to prove that he and no other slew the dragon, and grant him forgiveness and your peace."

The King reflected and did not hurry to respond. In mass the barons cried:

"Grant it, Sire, grant it!"

The King said: "I grant it." But Iseult knelt at his feet and said: "Father, first give me the kiss of peace and forgiveness, as a sign that you will give him the same."

Then she found Tristan and led him before the barony. And as he came the hundred knights rose all together, crossed their arms upon their breasts and bowed, and arrayed themselves beside him, so the Irish knew that he was their lord.

But among the Irish many knew him again and cried: "Tristan of Lyonesse that slew the Morholt!" They drew their swords and clamoured for death. But Iseult cried: "King, kiss this man upon the lips as your oath was," and the King kissed him, and the clamour fell.

Then Tristan showed the dragon's tongue and offered the seneschal battle, but the seneschal looked at his face and dared not.

Then Tristan said:

"My lords, you have said it, and it is truth: I killed the Morholt. But I crossed the sea to offer you a good blood-fine, to ransom that deed and get me quit of it.

"I put my body in peril of death and rid you of the beast and have so conquered Iseult the Fair, and having conquered her I will bear her away on my ship.

"But that these lands of Cornwall and Ireland may know no more hatred, but love only, learn that King Mark, my lord, will marry her. Here stand a hundred knights of high name, who all will swear with an oath upon the relics of the holy saints, that King Mark sends you by their embassy offer of peace and of brotherhood and goodwill; and that he would by your courtesy hold Iseult as his honoured wife, and that he would have all the men of Cornwall serve her as their Queen."

When the lords of Ireland heard this they acclaimed it, and the King also was content.

Then, since that treaty and alliance was to be made, the King her father took Iseult by the hand and asked of Tristan that he should take an oath; to wit that he would lead her loyally to his lord, and Tristan took that oath and swore it before the knights and the barony of Ireland assembled. Iseult the Fair trembled for shame and anguish. Thus Tristan, having won her, disdained her; the fine story of the hair of gold was but a lie; it was to another he was delivering her.

Then the King put Iseult's right hand into Tristan's right hand, and Tristan held it for a space in token of seizing for the King of Cornwall.

So, for the love of King Mark, did Tristan by guile and by force conquer the Queen of the Hair of Gold.

THE

PHILTRE

When the day of Iseult's livery to the lords of Cornwall drew near, her mother gathered herbs and flowers and roots and steeped them in wine, and brewed a potion of might, and having perfected it by science and magic, she poured it into a pitcher, and said apart to Brangien:

"Child, it is yours to go with Iseult to King Mark's country, for you love her with a faithful love. Take then this pitcher and remember well my words. Hide it so that no eye shall see nor no lip go near it: but when the wedding-night has come and that moment in which the wedded are left alone, pour this essenced wine into a cup and offer it to King Mark and to Iseult his Queen. Oh! Take all care, my child, that they alone shall taste this brew. For this is its power: they who drink of it together love each other with their every single sense and with their every thought, forever, in life and in death."

And Brangien promised the Queen that she would do her bidding.

The ship, ploughing the deep waves, bore off Iseult. The farther it bore her from the soil of Ireland, the more sadly the young girl bewailed her lot. Seated under the tent in which she had secluded herself with Brangien her maid, she wept, remembering her land. Where were these strangers dragging her? Towards whom? Towards what fate? When Tristan approached her and sought to soothe her with soft words, she angered, repulsed him, and hate swelled her heart. He had come to Ireland, he the ravisher, he the murderer of the Morholt; with guile he had torn her from her mother and her land; he had not deigned to keep her for himself, and now he was carrying her away as his prey, over the waves, to the land of the enemy. "Accursed be the sea that bears me, for rather would I lie dead on the earth where I was born than live out there, beyond. . . ."

One day when the wind had fallen and the sails hung slack Tristan dropped anchor by an island and the hundred knights of Cornwall and the sailors, weary of the sea, landed all. Iseult alone remained aboard and a little serving maid, when Tristan came near the Queen to calm her sorrow. The sun was hot above them and they were athirst and, as they called, the little maid looked about for drink for them and found that pitcher which the mother of Iseult had given into Brangien's keeping. And when she came on it, the child cried, "I have found you wine!" Now she had found not wine—but Passion and Joy most sharp, and Anguish without end, and Death.

The child filled a goblet and presented it to her mistress. The Queen drank deep of that draught and gave it to Tristan and he drank also long and emptied it all.

Brangien came in upon them; she saw them gazing at each other in silence as though ravished and apart; she saw the almost emptied pitcher standing there before them, and the goblet. She snatched up the pitcher and cast it into the shuddering sea and cried aloud: "Cursed be the day I was born and cursed the day that first I trod this deck. Iseult, my friend, and Tristan, you, you have drunk death together."

And once more the bark ran free for Tintagel. But it seemed to Tristan as though an ardent briar, sharp-thorned but with flower most sweet smelling drave roots into his blood and laced the lovely body of Iseult all round about it and bound it to his own and to his every thought and desire. And he thought: "Andret, Denoalen, Guenelon and Gondoïne, felons, that charged me with coveting King Mark's land, I have come lower by far, for it is not his land I covet. Fair uncle, who loved me orphaned ere ever you knew in me the blood of your sister Blanchefleur, you that wept as you bore me to that boat alone, why did you not drive out the boy that was to betray you? Ah! What thought was that! Iseult is yours and I am but your vassal; Iseult is yours and I am your son; Iseult is yours and may not love me."

But Iseult loved him, though she would have hated. Had he not basely disdained her? She could not hate, for a tenderness more sharp than hatred tore her.

And Brangien watched them in anguish, suffering more cruelly because she alone knew the depth of evil done.

Two days she watched them, seeing them refuse all food or comfort and seeking each other as blind men seek, wretched apart and together more wretched still, for then they trembled each for the first avowal.

On the third day, as Tristan neared the tent on deck where Iseult sat, she saw him coming and she said to him, very humbly, "Come in, my lord."

"Queen," said Tristan, "why do you call me lord? Am I not your liege and vassal, to revere and serve and cherish you as my lady and Queen?"

But Iseult answered, "No, you know that you are my lord and my master, and I your slave. Ah, why did I not sharpen those wounds of the wounded singer, or let die that dragon-slayer in the grasses of the marsh? Why did I not, while he lay helpless in the bath, plant on him the blow of the sword I brandished? But then I did not know what now I know!"

"And what is it that you know, Iseult? What is it that torments you?"

"Ah, all that I know torments me, and all that I see. This sky and this sea torment me, and my body and my life."

She laid her arm upon Tristan's shoulder, the light of her eyes was drowned and her lips trembled.

He repeated: "Friend, what is it that torments you?"

"The love of you," she said. Whereat he put his lips to hers.

But as they thus tasted their first joy, Brangien, that watched them, stretched her arms and cried at their feet in tears:

"Stay and return if still you can. . . . But oh! that path has no returning. For already Love and his strength drag you on and now henceforth forever never shall you know joy without pain again. The wine possesses you, the draught your mother gave me, the draught the King alone should have drunk with you: but that old Enemy has tricked us, all us three; it is you who have drained the goblet. Friend Tristan, Iseult my friend, for that bad ward I kept take here my body and my life for through me and in that cup, you have drunk not love alone, but love and death together."

The lovers held each other; life and desire trembled through their youth, and Tristan said, "Well then, come Death."

And as evening fell, upon the bark that heeled and ran to King Mark's land, they gave themselves up utterly to love.

BRANGIEN

DELIVERED

TO

THE

SERFS

As King Mark came down to greet Iseult upon the shore, Tristan took her hand and led her to the King and the King took seizing of her, taking her hand. He led her in great pomp to his castle of Tintagel, and as she came in hall amid the vassals her beauty shone so that the walls were lit as they are lit at dawn. Then King Mark blessed those swallows which, by happy courtesy, had brought the hair of gold, and Tristan also he blessed, and the hundred knights who, on that adventurous bark, had gone to find him joy of heart and of eyes; yet to him also that ship was to bring sting, torment and mourning.

And on the eighteenth day, having called his barony together he took Iseult to wife. But on the wedding night Brangien, to conceal the Queen's dishonour and save her from death, took her place in the nuptial couch. The loyal maid sacrificed the purity of her body to her friend, in remorse of the poor watch she had kept at sea, and out of love of Iseult. The darkness of the night hid her trick and her shame from the king.

Here the romancers insist that Brangien had not cast into the sea the flagon of spiced wine, which the lovers had not quite emptied; that, in the dawn, after her lady in turn had entered King Mark's bed, she poured into a cup what remained of the philtre and presented it to the pair; that Mark drank heavily of it and that Iseult secretly threw her share way.

But know, my lords, that these romancers have tampered with the tale and falsified it. They conceived this lie for the reason that they did not understand the marvellous love in which Mark ever held the Queen. In truth, as you shall see, never, despite anguish, torment and terrible reprisals, could Mark expel either Iseult or Tristan from his heart; yet know that he had not drunk the spiced wine. Neither poison nor sorcery, only the tender nobility of his heart, moved him to love.

Then Iseult lived as a queen, but lived in sadness. She had King Mark's tenderness and the barons' honour; the people also loved her; she passed her days amid the frescoes on the walls and floors all strewn with flowers; good jewels had she and purple cloth and tapestry of Hungary and Thessaly too, and songs of harpers, and curtains upon which were worked leopards and eagles and popinjays and all the beasts of sea and field. And her love too she had, love high and splendid, for as is the custom among great lords, Tristan could ever be near her. At his leisure and his dalliance, night and day: for he slept in the King's chamber as great lords do, among the lieges and the councillors. Yet still she feared; for though her love was secret and Tristan unsuspected (for who suspects a son?) Brangien knew. And Brangien seemed in the Queen's mind like a witness spying; for Brangien alone knew what manner of life she led, and held her at mercy so. And the Queen thought: "Ah, if some day she should weary of serving as a slave the bed where once she passed for Queen. . . . If Tristan should die from her betrayal!" So fear maddened the Queen, but not in truth the fear of Brangien who was loyal; her own heart bred the fear.

Hear now, my lords, the great treachery she planned; but God, as you shall see, had pity on her; be you also indulgent with her.

That day, Tristan and the King hunted afar, and Tristan knew nothing of this crime. Iseult had two serfs called before her, promised them freedom and sixty gold bezants if they swore to do her will. They swore an oath.

"I shall give you," said she, "a young girl; take her into the forest, it matters not whether far or near, but to some spot where none will ever learn what happened: there, kill her and bring me back her tongue. Remember, so that you can repeat them to me, the words which she will have said. Go now; when you return you will be freemen and rich."

Then she called Brangien. "Friend, you see how my body languishes and suffers: will you not go seek in the forest the plants which satisfy this sickness? Here are two serfs who will lead you; they know where the simples grow. So follow them; sister, know well that if I am sending you into the forest, it is for the sake of my peace and my life."

The serfs led her away. Once in the woods, she wished to stop, for the healing plants grew about her in abundance. But they led her ever farther: "Come, this is not the proper place."

One of the serfs strode before her, the other followed her. No more a beaten path, but brambles, thorns and tangling thistles. Suddenly the man who went before drew his sword and faced about; she turned to the other to seek help; he also held a naked sword by the hilt and said: "Young girl, we must kill you."

Brangien fell to the grass and with her arms sought to thrust the swordpoints aside. The voice in which she begged mercy of them was so piteous and soft that they said:

"Young girl, if Queen Iseult, your lady and ours, wishes that you die, doubtless it is because you have done her some great wrong."

She answered: "I know not, friends; I remember only one misdeed. When we left Ireland, each of us took with her, as the chief of her ornaments, a snow-white shift, a shift for her wedding night. On the sea it happened that Iseult tore her white shift, and for her wedding night I loaned her mine. Friends, that was the sole wrong I did her. Yet since it is her wish that I die, tell her that I send her greetings and love and that I thank her for all the goodness and honour she has shown me since as a child and stolen by pirates I was sold to her mother and placed in her service. May God in his goodness preserve her honour, her person, and her life. Brothers, now strike."

The serfs took pity. They held council and deciding that a misdeed such as hers perhaps did not merit death, they bound her to a tree. Then they killed a young dog: one of them cut out its tongue, tied it in the flap of his kirtle, and thus both reappeared before Iseult.

"Did she speak?" she inquired anxiously.

"Yes, Queen, she spoke. She said you were angered by a single wrong: that on the sea you had torn a snow-white shift which you had brought with you from Ireland, and on your wedding night she had loaned you hers. That, said she, was her only crime. She sent you thanks for many benefits received from you since childhood, she prayed God to protect your honour and your life. She sends you her greetings and her love. Queen, here is her tongue which we bring you."

"Murderers!" cried Iseult, "give me back Brangien, my beloved maid. Did you not know she was my only friend? Murderers, give her back to me!"

"Queen, it is said in sooth 'Woman changes in a few hours; in a single hour woman laughs, weeps, hates, loves.' We killed her, since you bade us to."

"How could I have bidden you? What wrong had there been: was she not my dear companion, sweet, loyal, beautiful? You knew it, murderers: I sent her to cull simples and confided her to your care that you might protect her on the way. But I shall say you killed her and you will be burned alive on coals."

"Queen, know that she is alive and that we will bring her back safe and sound to you."

But she did not believe them and like one deranged alternately cursed the murderers and herself. She had one of the serfs kept by her side while the other sped toward the tree to which Brangien was bound.

"Mistress, God has been merciful to you and your lady calls you back to her."

When she appeared before Iseult, Brangien knelt, begging her to pardon her her faults; but the Queen also fell to her knees before her, and, clasped in one another's arms, both swooned deeply away.

THE

TALL

PINE-TREE

Not Brangien who was faithful, not Brangein, but
themselves had these lovers to fear, for hearts so
stricken will lose their vigilance. Love pressed them
hard, as thirst presses the dying stag to the stream;
love dropped upon them from high heaven, as a
hawk slipped after long hunger falls right upon the
bird. And love will not be hidden. Brangien indeed
by her prudence saved them well, none ever surprised the Queen in her lover's arms. But in every
hour and place every man could see Love terrible,
that rode them, and could see in these lovers their

every sense overflowing like new wine working in the vat.

The four felons at court who had hated Tristan of old for his prowess, watched the Queen; they had guessed that great love, and they burnt with envy and hatred and now a kind of evil joy. They planned to give news of their watching to the King, to see his tenderness turned to fury, Tristan thrust out or slain, and the Queen in torment; for though they feared Tristan their hatred mastered their fear; and, on a day, the four barons called King Mark to parley, and Andret said:

"Fair King, your heart will be troubled and we four also mourn; yet are we bound to tell you what we know. You have placed your trust in Tristan and Tristan would shame you. In vain we warned you. For the love of one man you have mocked ties of blood and all your barony. Learn then that Tristan loves the Queen; it is truth proved and many a word is passing on it now."

The royal King shrank and answered:

"Coward! What thought was that? Indeed I have placed my trust in Tristan. And rightly, for on the day when the Morholt offered combat to you all, you hung your heads and were dumb, and you trembled before him; but Tristan dared him for the honour of this land, and took mortal wounds. Therefore do you hate him, and therefore do I cherish him beyond thee, Andret, and beyond any other; but what then have you seen or heard or known?"

"Naught, lord, save what your eyes could see or your ears hear. Look you and listen, Sire, if there is yet time."

And they left him to taste the poison.

King Mark could not shake off the evil spell. Contrary to his heart, in his turn he kept watch on his nephew, kept watch on the Queen; but Brangien noting it warned them both and the King watched in vain, so that, soon wearying of an ignoble task, but knowing (alas!) that he could not kill his uneasy thought, he sent for Tristan and said:

"Tristan, leave this castle; and having left it, remain apart and do not think to return to it, and do not repass its moat or boundaries. Felons have charged you with an awful treason, but ask me nothing; I could not speak their words without shame to us both, and for your part seek you no word to appease. I have not believed them . . . had I done so would I not long since have flung you to a shameful death? But their evil words have troubled all my soul and only by your absence can my disquiet be soothed. Go, doubtless I will soon recall you. Go, my son, you are still dear to me."

When the felons heard the news they said among themselves, "He is gone, the wizard; he is driven out. Surely he will cross the sea on far adventures to carry his traitor service to some distant king."

But Tristan had not strength to depart altogether; and when he had crossed the moats and boundaries of the castle he knew he could go no further. He stayed in Tintagel town and lodged with Gorvenal in a burgess' house, and languished oh! more wounded than when in that past day the shaft of the Morholt had tainted his body. Lately, when he had lain helpless in the hut built at the sea's edge and all had fled from the stench of his wounds, three men nevertheless attended him, Gorvenal, Dinas of Lidan and King Mark. Now, Gorvenal and Dinas still watched by his bed; but King Mark no longer came there, and Tristan groaned:

"In truth, fair uncle, my body now exhales the smell of a more repulsive poison, and your love no longer knows how to overcome your horror."

But in the fire of his fever, desire without redress bore him like a bolting horse towards the well-girdled towers which shut in the Queen; horse and rider broke upon the walls of stone; but horse and rider picked themselves up and ceaselessly threw themselves into the selfsame ride.

In the close towers Iseult the Fair drooped also, but more wretched still. For it was hers all day long to feign laughter and all night long to conquer fever and despair. And all night as she lay by King Mark's side, fever still kept her waking, and she stared at darkness. She longed to fly to Tristan and she dreamt dreams of running to the gates and of finding there sharp scythes, traps of the felons, that cut her tender knees; and she dreamt of weakness and falling, and that her wounds had left her blood upon the ground. Now these lovers would have died, but Brangien succoured them. At peril of her life she found the house where Tristan lay. There Gorvenal opened to her very gladly, knowing what salvation she could bring.

So she found Tristan, and to save the lovers she taught him a device, nor was ever known a more subtle ruse of love.

Behind the castle of Tintagel was an orchard fenced around and wide and all closed in with stout and pointed stakes and numberless trees were there and fruit on them, birds and clusters of sweet grapes. And furthest from the castle, by the stakes of the palisade, was a tall pine-tree, straight and with heavy branches spreading from its trunk. At its root a living spring welled calm into a marble round, then ran between two borders winding, throughout the orchard and so on, till it flowed at last within the castle and through the women's rooms.

And every evening, by Brangien's counsel, Tristan cut him twigs and bark, leapt the sharp stakes and, having come beneath the pine, threw them into the clear spring; they floated light as foam down the stream to the women's rooms; and Iseult watched for their coming, and on those evenings she would wander out into the orchard and find her friend. Lithe and in fear would she come, watching at every step for what might lurk in the trees observing, foes or the felons whom she knew. Tristan, as soon as he saw her, would spring towards her with outspread arms. And the night and the branches of the pine protected them.

And so she said one night: "Oh, Tristan, I have heard that the castle is fairy and that twice a year it vanishes away. So is it vanished now and this is that enchanted orchard of which the harpers sing. A wall of air girdles it on all sides; there are flowering trees, a balmy soil; here without vigil the hero lives in his friend's arms and no hostile force can shatter the wall of air."

Even as she spoke, from the towers of Tintagel there resounded the bugles of sentinels announcing the dawn.

"No," said Tristan, "the wall of air already lies shattered and this is not the enchanted orchard. But, one day, friend, we shall go together to a fortunate land from which none returns. There, rises a castle of white marble; at each of its thousand windows burns a lighted candle; at each a minstrel plays and sings a melody without end; the sun does not shine there but none regrets his light: it is the happy land of the living."

But high on the towers of Tintagel the dawn illuminated alternate great blocks of vert and azure.

Iseult had refound her joy. Mark's thought of ill-ease grew faint; but the felons felt or knew which way lay truth, and they guessed that Tristan had met the Queen. Till at last Duke Andret (whom God shame) said to his peers:

"My lords, let us take counsel of Frocin the dwarf; for he knows the seven arts, and magic and every kind of charm. At the birth of a child he knows so well to observe the seven planets and the courses of the stars that he can foretell the events of his life. By the power of Bugibus and of Noiron he can discover hidden things. He will teach us if he will the wiles of Iseult the Fair."

In hate of beauty and of prowess, the little evil man drew signs for them and characters of sorcery; he cast the fortunes of the hour and then at last he said:

"Sirs, high good lords, this night shall you seize them both."

Then they led the little wizard to the King, and he said:

"Sire, bid your huntsmen leash the hounds and saddle the horses, proclaim a seven days' hunt in the forest and seven nights abroad therein, and hang me high if you do not hear this night what converse Tristan holds."

So did the King unwillingly; and at fall of night he left the hunt taking the dwarf in pillion, and entered the orchard, and the dwarf took him to the tall pine-tree, saying:

"Fair King, climb into these branches and take with you your arrows and your bow, for you may need them; and bide you still. You will not have long to wait."

"Begone, dog of the Evil One!" answered Mark.

And the dwarf departed, taking the horse.

He had spoken truly; the King did not wait long. That night the moon shone clear. Hid in the branches the King saw his nephew leap the palisades and throw his bark and twigs into the stream. But Tristan had bent over the round well to throw them and so doing had seen the image of the King. He could not stop the branches as they floated away, and there, yonder, in the women's rooms, Iseult was watching and would come. May God protect the lovers!

She came, and Tristan watched her motionless. Above him in the tree he heard the click of the arrow when it fits the string.

She came, but lightly and carefully, as was her wont, thinking: "What has passed, that Tristan does not come to meet me? He has seen some foe."

She stopped short, scanned with a glance the thick black wood. Suddenly, by the clear moonshine, she also saw the King's shadow in the fount. She showed the wit of women well, she did not lift her eyes.

"Lord God," she said, low down, "grant I may be the first to speak."

She drew still closer. Hear how she overtook and warned her friend:

"Tristan," she said, "what have you dared to do, calling me hither at such an hour? Often have you called me—to beseech, you said. And Queen though

I am, I know you won me that title—and I have
come. What would you?"

"Queen, I would have you pray the King for me."

She was in tears and trembling, but Tristan
praised God the Lord who had shown his friend her
peril.

"Queen," he went on, "often and in vain have I
summoned you; never since the King drove me away
have you deigned to come at my call. Take pity; the
King hates me and I know not why. Perhaps you
know the cause and can charm his anger. For whom
can he trust if not you, chaste Queen and courteous,
Iseult?"

"Truly, Lord Tristan, you do not know he doubts
us both. And I, to add to my shame, must acquaint
you of it. Ah! My lord believes I love you with a
guilty love. God nonetheless knows, and if I lie, may
He cover my body with disgrace, that I have never
given my love to any man saving only him who first
took me, a maiden, into his arms. And would you
have me, at such a time, implore your pardon of the
King? Why, did he know of my passage here tonight
he would cast my ashes to the wind."

Tristan groaned:

"Fair uncle, the world says 'No man is villainous if
he commits no villainy.' But in what manner of
heart could such a suspicion arise?"

"Sir Tristan, what do you mean? No, the King my
lord would not of himself have conceived such villainy. But the felons of this land made him believe
this lie, for it is easy to deceive the loyal heart. 'They
love each other,' they told him, and the felons
charged us with crime. Yes, you love me, Tristan,
why deny it? Am I not your uncle's wife and did I
not twice save you from death? Yes, I love you in

return for are you not of the royal blood and have I not oftentimes heard my mother declare that no woman loves her lord so long as she does not love his kin. It is for love of the King that I love you, Tristan; from this time forth, should he take you into grace again, I would be happy. My body trembles and I am afraid. I go, for I have waited too long."

In the branches the King smiled and had pity.

And as Iseult fled: "Queen," said Tristan, "in the Lord's name help me, for charity. The cowards would remove from the King's side all those who love him; they have succeeded and now mock him. So be it; I will go from this land, far away, poor as I once came into it: but at the very least, do you prevail upon the King that in recognition of past services, so that I can ride into other countries without shame, he give me enough of his goods to discharge my obligations, to redeem my horse and arms."

"No, Tristan, you should not have made this request of me. I am alone in this land, alone in this palace where none loves me, unsupported, at the mercy of the King. Do you not see that should I say a word for you to him, I would risk a shameful death? Friend, God aid you! The King wrongs you but the Lord God will be by you in whatever land you go."

So she went back to the women's rooms and told it to Brangien, who cried: "Iseult, God has worked a miracle for you, for he is compassionate and will not hurt the innocent in heart."

Under the tall pine-tree, Tristan, leaning against the rim of marble, bemoaned his fate:

"May God have pity on me and repair the great injustice which I suffer from my dear lord."

And when he had left the orchard, the King said smiling:

"Fair nephew, blessed be this hour. Only see: that long ride you planned this morning is over now."

But in an open glade apart, Frocin, the dwarf, read in the clear stars that the King now meant his death; he blackened with shame and fear and fled into Wales.

THE

DWARF

FROCIN

King Mark made peace with Tristan. Tristan returned to the castle as of old. Tristan slept in the King's chamber with his peers. He could come or go, the King thought no more of it. But who can long keep his love a secret? Love alas cannot be hid.

Mark pardoned the felons, and as the seneschal, Dinas of Lidan, found the dwarf wandering in a forest abandoned, he brought him home, and the King had pity and pardoned even him.

But his goodness did but feed the ire of the

barons, who freshly having surprised Tristan and the Queen swore this oath: If the King kept Tristan in the land they would withdraw to their strongholds as for war, and they called the King to parley.

"Lord," said they, "love us, hate us, as you will, but we desire that you drive Tristan forth. He loves the Queen as all who choose can see, but as for us we will bear it no longer."

And the King sighed, looking down in silence.

"King," they went on, "we will not bear it, for we know now that this is known to you and that yet you will not move. Parley you, and take counsel. As for us if you will not exile this man, your nephew, and drive him forth out of your land forever, we will withdraw within our bailiwicks and take our neighbours also from your court: for we cannot endure his presence longer in this place. Such is your balance: choose."

"My lords," said he, "once I hearkened to the evil words you spoke of Tristan, yet was I wrong in the end. But you are my lieges and I would not lose the service of my men. Counsel me therefore, I charge you, you that owe me counsel. You know me for a man neither proud nor overstepping."

"Lord," said they, "call then Frocin hither. You mistrust him for that orchard night. Still, was it not he that read in the stars of the Queen's coming there and to the very pine-tree too? He is very wise, take counsel of him."

And he came, did that hunchback of Hell: the felons greeted him and he planned this evil.

"Sire," said he, "let your nephew ride hard to-morrow at dawn with a brief drawn up on parchment and well sealed with a seal: bid him ride to King

Arthur at Carduel. Sire, he sleeps with the peers in your chamber; go you out when the first sleep falls on men, and if he love Iseult so madly, why, then I swear by God and by the laws of Rome, he will try to speak with her before he rides. But if he do so unknown to you or to me, then slay me. As for the trap, let me lay it, but do you say nothing of his ride to him until the time for sleep."

And when King Mark had agreed, this dwarf did a vile thing. He bought of a baker four farthings' worth of flour, and hid it in the turn of his coat. That night, when the King had supped and the men-at-arms lay down to sleep in hall, Tristan came to the King as custom was, and the King said:

"Fair nephew, do my will: ride to-morrow night to King Arthur at Carduel, and give him this brief, with my greeting, that he may open it: and stay you with him but one day."

And when Tristan said: "I will take it on the morrow"; the King added: "Aye, and before day dawn."

But, as the peers slept all round the King their lord, that night, a mad thought took Tristan that, before he rode, he knew not for how long, before dawn he would say a last word to the Queen. And there was a spear length in the darkness between them. Now the dwarf slept with the rest in the King's chamber, and when he thought that all slept he rose and scattered the flour silently in the spear length that lay between the bed of Tristan and that of the Queen. Should one of the lovers go to join the other, the flour would retain the imprint of his steps. But as he strewed it about, Tristan, who lay awake, saw him: "What does this mean? This dwarf is not in the habit of working for my weal, but he shall be deceived: only a fool would let him take the imprint of his steps."

At midnight, when all was dark in the room, no candle nor any lamp glimmering, the King went out silently by the door and with him the dwarf. Then Tristan rose in the darkness and judged the spear length and leapt the space between, for his farewell. But that day in the hunt a boar had wounded him in the leg, and to his bad luck the wound was unbandaged, and in this effort bled. He did not feel it or see it in the darkness, but the blood dripped upon the couches and the floor strewn between; and outside in the moonlight the dwarf read the heavens and knew that the lovers were together. He trembled with joy at the thought and cried:

"Enter, my King, and if you do not find them together, hang me high!"

Then the King and the dwarf and the four felons ran in with lights and noise, and though Tristan had regained his place there was the blood for witness, and though Iseult feigned sleep, and Perinis too, who lay at Tristan's feet, yet there was the blood for witness. And the King looked in silence at the blood where it lay upon the bed and the boards and trampled into the floor.

And the four barons held Tristan down upon his bed and mocked the Queen also, promising her full justice; and they bared and showed the wound whence the blood flowed.

Then the King said:

"Tristan, now nothing longer holds. To-morrow you shall die."

And Tristan answered:

"Have mercy, lord, in the name of God that suffered the cross!"

But the felons called on the King to take vengeance, saying:

"Do justice, King: take vengeance."

And Tristan went on, "Have mercy, not on me—for why should I stand at dying?—Truly, but for you, I would have sold my honour high to cowards who, under your peace, have put hands on my body—but in homage to you I have yielded and you may do with me what you will. But, lord, remember the Queen!"

And as he knelt at the King's feet he still complained:

"Remember the Queen; for if any man of your household make so bold as to maintain the lie that I loved her unlawfully, I will stand up armed to him in a ring. Sire, in the name of God the Lord, have mercy on her."

Then the barons bound him with ropes, and the Queen also. But had Tristan known that trial by combat was to be denied him, certainly he would not have suffered it.

For he trusted in God and knew no man dared draw sword against him in the lists. And truly he did well to trust in God, for though the felons mocked him when he said he had loved loyally, yet I call you to witness, my lords who read this, and who know of the philtre drunk upon the high seas, and who understand whether his love were disloyalty indeed. For men see this and that outward thing, but God alone the heart, and in the heart alone is Crime and the sole final judge is God. Therefore did He lay down the law that a man accused might uphold his cause by battle, and God himself fights for the innocent in such a combat.

Therefore did Tristan claim justice and the right

of battle and therefore was he careful to fail in nothing of the homage he owed King Mark, his lord.

But had he known what was coming, he would
have killed the felons. Lord God, why did he not kill
them!

THE

CHANTRY

LEAP

Dark was the night, and the news ran that Tristan and the Queen were held and that the King would kill them; and wealthy burgess, or common man, they wept and ran to the palace.

"Alas, well must we weep! Tristan, fearless baron, must you die by such shabby treachery? And you, loyal and honoured Queen, in what land was ever born a king's daughter so beautiful, so dear? Is this, humped-back dwarf, the work of your auguries? May he never see the face of God who, having found you, does not drive his spear into your body!

Tristan, fair dear friend, when the Morholt, come to ravish our children, set foot on these shores, not one of our barons dared arm himself against him, and all were silent like mutes. But you, Tristan, you fought for us, the men of Cornwall, and you slew the Morholt; and he struck you a wound with his spear of which you almost died for us. To-day, in memory of these things, can we consent in your death?"

And the murmurs and the cries ran through the city, but such was the King's anger in his castle above that not the strongest nor the proudest baron dared move him.

Night ended and the day drew near. Mark, before dawn, rode out to the place where he held pleas and judgment. He ordered a ditch to be dug in the earth and knotty vine-shoots and thorns to be laid therein.

At the hour of Prime he had a ban cried through his land to gather the men of Cornwall; they came with a great noise and none but did weep saving only the dwarf of Tintagel. The King spoke them thus:

"My lords, I have made here a faggot of thorns for Tristan and the Queen; for they have fallen."

But they cried all, with tears:

"A sentence, lord, a sentence; an indictment and pleas; for killing without trial is shame and crime. King, respite and mercy for them!"

But Mark answered in his anger:

"Neither respite, nor delay, nor pleas, nor sentence. By God that made the world, if any dare petition me, he shall burn first!"

He ordered the fire to be lit, and Tristan to be called.

The flames rose, and all were silent before the flames, and the King waited.

The servants ran to the room where watch was

kept on the two lovers; and they dragged Tristan by his hands which were bound with ropes. By God it was vile to fetter him thus! He wept at the insult, but of what use were his tears? Ignominiously they marched him off, and the Queen called after him, almost demented with anguish:

"To be killed, friend, that you might live, that would be great joy!"

The guards and Tristan went down from the city towards the stake. But, behind them, a knight galloped up and joined them: it was Dinas the good seneschal. At the news of the misfortune, he had come from his castle of Lidan, and foam, sweat and blood streamed from his horse's flanks:

"Son, I haste towards the King's sitting. God there perhaps will grant me to hit upon some plan that will help both of you; already he permits me to serve you by a slight act of courtesy. Friends," he said to the servants, "I wish you to lead him without these fetters." And Dinas cut the shameful ropes. "Should he try to flee, do you not have your swords?"

He kissed Tristan on the lips, sprang into his saddle, and his horse bore him off.

Now, hear how full of pity is God. He who does not desire the sinner's death heard the lament and the prayers of the common folk, beseeching him for the tormented lovers. Near the road where Tristan passed was a chantry upon a rock. It stood at a cliff's edge steep and sheer, and it turned to the sea-breeze; in the apse of it were windows of stained glass, the skilful work of a saint. Then Tristan said to those with him:

"My lords, see you this chantry? Permit me to enter it. My death is near, I shall ask God that he have mercy on me, who so offended him. There is but one door to the place, my lords, and each of you has his sword drawn. So, you may well see that, when my prayer to God is done, I must come past you again: when I have prayed God, my lords, for the last time."

And one of the guards said:

"Why, let him go in."

So they let him enter to pray. But he, once in, dashed through and leapt the altar rail and the altar too and forced a window of the apse, and leapt again over the cliff's edge. So might he die, but not of that shameful death before the people.

Now learn, my lords, how generous was God to him that day. The wind took Tristan's cloak and he fell upon a smooth rock at the cliff's foot, which to this day the men of Cornwall call "Tristan's leap."

His guards still waited for him at the chantry door, but vainly, for God was now his guard. And he ran, and the fine sand crunched under his feet, and far off he saw the faggot burning, and the smoke and the crackling flames; and fled.

Sword girt and bridle loose, Gorvenal had fled the city, lest the King burn him in his master's place: and he found Tristan on the shore.

"Master," said Tristan, "God has saved me, but oh! master, to what end? For without Iseult I may not and I will not live, and I rather had died of my fall. I have escaped, Iseult, and they will kill you. They will burn her for me, then I too will die for her."

"Lord," said Gorvenal, "take no counsel of anger. See here this thicket with a ditch dug round about it. Let us hide therein where the track passes near, and comers by it will tell us news; and, boy, if they burn Iseult, I swear by God, the Son of Mary, never to sleep under a roof again until she be avenged."

"Good master, I have not got my sword."

"Here, I have brought it to you."

"Well done, master; I fear nothing now, save God."

"Son, under my tunic I have something else which will rejoice you: this light and solid coat of mail, which may come handy."

"Give it me, fair master. By the God in whom I believe, I go now to free my friend."

"No, do not hurry," said Gorvenal. "God without doubt has reserved some surer vengeance for you. But think that it is not in your power to approach the stake; the burghers surround it and fear the King: the very man who wishes your freedom will be the first to strike you. Son, it is well said 'Folly is not prowess.' Wait. . . ."

There was a poor man of the common folk that had seen Tristan's fall, and had seen him stumble and rise after, and he crept to Tintagel and to Iseult where she was bound, and said:

"Queen, weep no more. Your friend has fled safely."

"Then I thank God," said she, "and whether they bind or loose me, and whether they kill or spare me, I care but little now."

And though blood came at the cord's-knots, so tightly had the traitors bound her, yet still she said, smiling:

"Did I weep for that when God has loosed my friend I should be little worth."

When the news came to the King that Tristan had

leapt that leap and was lost he paled with anger, and bade his men bring forth Iseult.

They dragged her from the room, and she came before the crowd, held by her delicate hands, from which blood dropped, and the crowd called:

"Have pity on her—the loyal Queen and honoured! Surely they that gave her up brought mourning on us all—our curses on them!"

But the King's men dragged her to the thorn faggot as it blazed.

Then Dinas, Lord of Lidan, knelt before the King.

"Sire, hear me; I have served you many years, without stint and loyally, without benefit to myself, for there is no poor man nor orphan nor old woman who would give me a penny for your stewardship, which I have held all my life. In reward, grant me your mercy for the Queen. You wish to burn her without trial: that is malfeasance, since she has not acknowledged the crime of which you accuse her. Think, too. If you burn her body, there will no longer be safety in your lands: Tristan has escaped; well does he know the plains, the woods, the fords, the ways, and he is fearless. Most certainly, you are his uncle and he will not lay hand on you; but every baron, every vassal he chances upon, he will kill."

The four felons blanched to hear him: already they saw Tristan in ambush, lying in wait for them.

"King," said the seneschal, "since it is true that I have served you well all my life, yield Iseult to me: I will answer for her as her guard and her warrantor."

But the King took Dinas by the hand and swore by the names of the saints forthwith to do justice.

Dinas arose:

"King, I am going back to Lidan and I cast off your service."

Iseult smiled sadly at him. He mounted his charger and rode away, sorry, bowed and dejected.

Iseult stood up before the flame, and the crowd cried its anger and cursed the traitors and the King. None could see her without pity, unless he had a felon's heart: she was so tightly bound. The tears ran down her face and fell upon her grey gown where ran a little thread of gold, and a thread of gold was twined into her hair.

Just then there had come up a hundred lepers, deformed men with pitted and livid faces, limping on crutches to the clatter of hand-rattles. They crowded to the stake, and under their swollen eyelids, their blood-shot eyes gleamed at the sight. Yvain, the ugliest of them all, cried to the King in a piercing voice:

"O King, you would burn this woman in that flame, and it is sound justice, but too swift, for very soon the fire will fall, and her ashes will very soon be scattered by the high wind and her agony be done. Would you have me show you a worse punishment, by which she would live, but in great shame and ever desiring death? Would you, King?"

"Yes, life then for her, but in great shame and worse than death—I could love him who showed me such a torture."

"Sire, in a few words here is my thought. See, I have a hundred comrades here. Give Iseult to us, so that we may have her in common. Our sickness fans our desires. Give her to your lepers: never will a lady have come to a worse end. See, our rags stick to our sores that ooze. She who at your side delighted in rich stuffs trimmed with fur, in jewels, in halls decked with marble, she who enjoyed fine wines, marks of esteem and merriments, when she beholds the court of your lepers, when she has to enter our hovels and lie with us, then Iseult the Fair, the Beautiful, will recognize her sin and will regret this fine black-thorn fire."

And as the King heard them, he stood a long time without moving; then he ran to the Queen and seized her by the hand, and she cried:

"Burn me! rather burn me!"

But the King gave her up, and Yvain took her, and the hundred lepers pressed around. At the sound of their cries and yelpings, all hearts melted for pity. But Yvain had an evil gladness, and as he went he dragged her out of the borough bounds, with his hideous company.

Now they took that road where Tristan lay in hiding, and Gorvenal said to him:

"Son, here is your friend. Will you do naught?"

Then Tristan mounted the horse and spurred it out of the bush, and cried:

"Yvain, you have been at the Queen's side a moment, and too long. Now leave her if you would live."

But Yvain threw his cloak away and shouted:

"Your clubs, comrades, and your staves! Crutches in the air—for a fight is on!"

Then it was fine to see the lepers throwing their capes aside, and stirring their sick legs, and brandishing their crutches, some threatening: groaning all; but to strike them Tristan was too noble. There are singers who sing that Tristan killed Yvain, but it is a lie. Too much a knight was he to kill such things.

Gorvenal indeed, snatching up an oak sapling, crashed it on Yvain's head till his blood ran down to his misshapen feet. Then Tristan took the Queen.

Henceforth near him she felt no further evil. He cut the cords that bound her arms so straightly, and he left the plain so that they plunged into the wood of Morois; and there in the thick wood Tristan was as sure as in a castle keep.

And as the sun fell they halted all three at the foot of a little hill: fear had wearied the Queen, and she leant her head upon his body and slept.

But in the morning, Gorvenal stole from a woodman his bow and two good arrows plumed and barbed, and gave them to Tristan, the great archer, and he shot him a fawn and killed it. Then Gorvenal gathered dry twigs, struck flint, and lit a great fire to cook the venison. And Tristan cut him branches and made a hut and garnished it with leaves. And Iseult slept upon the thick leaves there.

So, in the depths of the wild wood began for the lovers that savage life which yet they loved very soon.

THE

WOOD

OF

MOROIS

They wandered in the depths of the wild wood, rest-less and in haste like beasts that are hunted, nor did they often dare to return by night to the shelter of yesterday. They ate but the flesh of wild animals, and missed the taste of salt. Their faces sank and grew white, their clothes ragged, for the briars tore them. They loved each other and they did not know that they suffered.

One day, as they were wandering in these high woods that had never yet been felled or ordered, they came upon the hermitage of Ogrin.

The old man limped in the sunlight under a light growth of maples near his chapel: he leant upon his crutch, and cried:

"Lord Tristan, hear the great oath which the Cornish men have sworn. The King has published a ban in every parish: Whosoever may seize you shall receive a hundred marks of gold for his guerdon, and all the barons have sworn to give you up alive or dead. Do penance, Tristan! God pardons the sinner who turns to repentance."

"And of what should I repent, Ogrin, my lord? Or of what crime? You that sit in judgment upon us here, do you know what cup it was we drank upon the high sea? That good, great draught inebriates us both. I would rather beg my life long and live of roots and herbs with Iseult than, lacking her, be king of a wide kingdom."

"God aid you, Lord Tristan; for you have lost both this world and the next. A man that is traitor to his lord is worthy to be torn by horses and burnt upon the faggot, and wherever his ashes fall no grass shall grow and all tillage is waste, and the trees and the green things die. Lord Tristan, give back the Queen to the man who espoused her lawfully according to the laws of Rome."

"She is no longer his. He gave her to his lepers. From these lepers I myself conquered her with my own hand; and henceforth she is altogether mine. She cannot pass from me nor I from her."

Ogrin sat down; but at his feet Iseult, her head upon the knees of that man of God, wept silently. The hermit told her and re-told her the words of his holy book, but still while she wept she shook her head, and refused the faith he offered.

"Ah me," said Ogrin then, "what comfort can one

give the dead? Do penance, Tristan, for a man who lives in sin without repenting is a man quite dead."

"Oh no," said Tristan, "I live and I do no penance. We will go back into the high wood which comforts and wards us all round about. Come with me, Iseult, my friend."

Iseult rose up; they held each other's hands. They passed into the high grass and the underwood: the trees hid them with their branches. They disappeared beyond the curtain of the leaves.

Hear now, my lords, a good adventure. Tristan had reared a dog, a greyhound, fine, keen, fleet of foot: no count or king had a better for the chase with bows. He was called Hodain. It had been necessary to shut him in the donjon, fettered by a block hung to his neck: since the day he had ceased seeing his master he had rejected every scrap of food, scratched the earth with his paw, wept from his eyes and howled. Many had pity on him:

"Hodain," said they, "no animal ever has loved better than you: yes, Solomon wisely said 'My true friend is my greyhound.' "

And King Mark, recalling past days, thought in his heart:

"This dog shows wisdom in mourning for his master thus; for in all Cornwall is there anyone worth Tristan?"

Three barons came to the King:

"Sire, have Hodain unchained: well we know that his grief is caused by the loss of his master; if you do not, you will see him, as soon as he is set free, chasing men and beasts with open maw and hanging tongue, to rend them."

They unchained him. He sprang out of the door and to the chamber where he lately used to find

Tristan. He growled, wailed, hunted about, at last discovered his master's scent. Step by step he traversed the road by which Tristan had gone to the stake. All followed him. He yelped distinctly and climbed towards the cliff. Inside the chantry, he sprang on the altar; suddenly he leaped through the window in the apse, fell to the foot of the rock, on the sands recovered the trail, pointed an instant in the flowering copse where Tristan had concealed himself, then raced towards the forest. No one present was unmoved by the sight.

"Fair King," now said the knights, "let us not follow him; he might lead us to a spot whence it might be difficult to return."

They let him be and turned about. In the coverts the dog bayed, and the forest echoed with the sound. From afar, Tristan, the Queen and Gorvenal heard it: "It is Hodain!" They took fright: they thought the King was hunting them, tracking them down like beasts with his greyhounds. . . . They buried themselves in a thicket. At its edge Tristan stood ready with bent bow. But no sooner had Hodain seen and recognized his master than he sprang to him, wagged his head and his tail, arched his back and cast himself in circles on the ground. Whoever saw such joy? Then he ran to Iseult the Fair, to Gorvenal, and also welcomed the horse. Tristan was deeply moved:

"Alas, by what ill fortune has he found us? Of what use is this dog, who cannot keep silent, to a harassed man? The King is beating plains and woods, all his lands, for us: Hodain will betray us with his bayings. It was for love of me, that in his noble nature he came to seek his death. Nevertheless we must protect ourselves. What is to be done? Give me your counsel."

Iseult stroked Hodain and said:

"Sire, spare him! I have heard tell of a Welsh woodman who had trained his dog to follow without barking the blood-trails of wounded stags. Friend Tristan, what joy it would be if in taking pains one could thus train Hodain."

For a while he hesitated, while the dog licked the hands of Iseult. Moved, Tristan said:

"I will try; I cannot bear to kill him."

Shortly, Tristan went hunting, started a buck, wounded him with an arrow. The dog darted on the buck's trail and barked so loudly that the woods re-echoed. Tristan silenced him by striking him; Hodain lifted his head towards his master in astonishment, dared not bark and dropped the pursuit; Tristan then took him between his knees and beat his own boot with his stick of chestnut-wood, as do the huntsmen to excite the dogs. At the signal Hodain again started to bark and Tristan again chastised him. Teaching him in this way at the end of scarcely a month he had trained him to hunt in silence: when his arrow had wounded a fallow deer or roebuck, without a sound Hodain followed the trace over snow, over ice or turf; if he found the beast in a covert the dog knew enough to mark the spot by dragging boughs to it; if in the open, he laid grass on the fallen body and returned without a bark to find his master.

The summer passed and the winter came: the two lovers lived, all hidden in the hollow of a rock, and on the frozen earth the cold crisped their couch with dead leaves. In the strength of their love neither one nor the other felt these mortal things. But when the open skies had come back with the springtime, they built a hut of green branches under the great trees. Tristan had known, ever since his childhood, that art by which a man may sing the song of birds in the woods, and at his fancy, he would call as call the thrush, the blackbird and the nightingale, and all winged things; and sometimes in reply very many birds would come on to the branches of his hut and sing their song full-throated in the new light.

The lovers had ceased to wander through the forest, for none of the barons ran the risk of their pursuit knowing well that Tristan would have hanged them to the branches of a tree. One day, however, one of the four traitors, Guenelon, whom God blast! drawn by the heat of the hunt, dared enter the Morois. And that morning, on the forest edge in a ravine, Gorvenal, having unsaddled his horse, had let him graze on the new grass, while far off in their hut Tristan held the Queen, and they slept. Then suddenly Gorvenal heard the cry of the pack; the hounds pursued a deer, which fell into that ravine. And far on the heath the hunter showed—and Gorvenal knew him for the man whom his master hated above all. Alone, with bloody spurs, and striking his horse's mane, he galloped on; but Gorvenal watched him from ambush: he came fast, he would return more slowly. He passed and Gorneval leapt from his ambush and seized the rein and, suddenly, remembering all the wrong that man had done, hewed him to death and carried off his head in his hands. And when the hunters found the body, as they followed, they thought Tristan came after and they fled in fear of death, and thereafter no man hunted in that wood. And far off, in the hut upon their couch of leaves, slept Tristan and the Queen in one another's arms.

There came Gorvenal, noiseless, the dead man's head in his hands that he might lift his master's heart at his awakening. He hung it by its hair outside the hut, and the leaves garlanded it about. Tristan woke and saw it, half hidden in the leaves, and staring at him as he gazed, and he became afraid. But Gorvenal said: "Fear not, he is dead. I killed him with this sword. He was your foe."

Then Tristan was glad, and from that day no one dared enter the wild wood, for terror guarded it and the lovers were lords of it all: and then it was that Tristan fashioned his bow "Failnaught" which struck home always, man or beast, whatever it aimed at.

My lords, upon a summer day, when mowing is, a little after Whitsuntide, as the birds sang dawn Tristan left his hut and girt his sword on him, and took his bow "Failnaught" and went off to hunt in the wood; but before evening, great evil was to fall on him, for no lovers ever loved so much or paid their love so dear.

When Tristan came back, broken by the heat, he embraced the Queen.

"Friend, where have you been?"

"Hunting a hart," he said, "that wearied me. I would lie down and sleep."

So she lay down, and he, and between them Tristan put his naked sword. To their good fortune they had kept on their clothes. On the Queen's finger was that ring of gold with emeralds set therein, which Mark had given her on her bridal day; but her hand was so wasted that the ring hardly held. Thus they slept, one of Tristan's arms beneath the neck of his friend, the other stretched over her fair body, close together; only their lips did not touch. And no wind blew, and no leaves stirred, but through a crevice in the branches a sunbeam fell upon the face of Iseult, and it shone white like ice. Now a woodman found in the wood a place where the leaves were crushed, where the lovers had halted and slept, and he followed their track and found the hut, and saw them sleeping and fled off, fearing the terrible awakening of that lord. He fled to Tintagel, and going up the stairs of the palace, found the King as he held his pleas in hall amid the vassals assembled.

"Friend," said the King, "what came you hither to seek in haste and breathless, like a huntsman that has followed the dogs afoot? Have you some wrong to right, or has any man driven you?"

But the woodman took him aside and said low down:

"I have seen the Queen and Tristan, and I feared and fled."

"Where saw you them?"

"In a hut in Morois, they slept side by side. Come swiftly and take your vengeance."

"Go," said the King, "and await me at the forest edge where the Red Cross stands, and tell no man what you have seen. You shall have gold and silver at your will."

The woodman went and sat himself beneath the Red Cross. God's curse on the spy! But he was to die miserably, as this story shortly will show.

The King had saddled his horse and girt his sword and left the city alone, and as he rode alone he minded him of the night when he had seen Tristan under the great pine-tree, and Iseult with her clear face, and he thought:

"If I find them I will avenge this awful wrong."

At the foot of the Red Cross he came to the woodman and said:

"Go first, and lead me straight and quickly."

The dark shade of the great trees wrapt them round, and as the King followed the spy he felt his sword, and trusted it for the great blows it had struck of old; and surely had Tristan wakened, one of the two had stayed there dead. Then the woodman said:

"King, we are near."

He held the stirrup, and tied the rein to a green apple-tree, and saw in a sunlit glade the hut with its flowers and leaves. Then the King cast his cloak with its fine buckle of gold and his tall frame grew plain. Drawing his sword from its sheath he said again in his heart that they or he should die. And he signed to the woodman to be gone.

He came alone into the hut, sword bare, and watched them as they lay: but he saw that they were apart, and he wondered because between them was the naked blade.

Then he said to himself: "My God, I may not kill them. For all the time they have lived together in this wood, had it been with a mad love that they loved each other, would they have placed this sword between them? Does not all the world know that a naked sword separating two bodies is the proof and the guardian of chastity? If they loved each other with mad love, would they lie here so purely? No, I will not slay, for that would be treason and wrong; and if I wakened this sleeper and one of us twain were killed, men would speak long of it and to our dishonour. But I will do so that when they wake they may know that I found them here, asleep, and spared them and that God had pity on them both."

And still the sunbeam fell upon the white face of Iseult, and the King took his ermined gloves: "It was she," thought he, "who lately brought them to me from Ireland," and put them up against the crevice whence it shone. Then he softly withdrew the emerald ring which he had given the Queen; at that time he had had to press on it to slip it on her finger; now her fingers were so thin that the ring came easily. In its place the King put the ring which Iseult once had given him. Then he took up the sword which separated the lovers, the very one—he recognized it—which had splintered in the skull of the Morholt; put his own in its place, quit the hut, leaped into the saddle and said to the woodman:

"Flee now and save your hide if you can!"

Then in her sleep a vision came to Iseult. She seemed to be in a great wood and two lions near her fought for her, and she gave a cry and woke, and the gloves fell upon her breast; and at the cry Tristan woke, and made to seize his sword, and saw by the golden hilt that it was the King's. And the Queen saw on her finger the King's ring, and she cried:

"Oh, my lord, woe is us! The King has found us here!"

And Tristan said:

"He has taken my sword; he was alone, he took fright and has gone for succour; he will return, and will burn us before the people. Let us fly."

So by great marches with Gorvenal alone they fled towards Wales, to the very edge of the wood of Morois. What sorrows love shall have caused them!

OGRIN

THE

HERMIT

After three days it happened that Tristan, in following a wounded deer far out into the wood, was caught by nightfall, and took to thinking thus under the dark wood alone:

"It was not fear that moved the King . . . he had my sword and I slept, I was at his mercy, he could have struck . . . he needed no succour. And if he wished to take me alive, why, having disarmed me, should he have left me his own sword? Oh, my father, my father, I know you now. There was pardon in your heart, and tenderness and pity . . . yet how was that, for who could forgive in this matter without shame . . . ? It was not pardon, it was understanding; the faggot and the chantry leap and the leper ambush have shown him God upon our side. Also I think he remembered the boy who long ago harped at his feet, and my land of Lyonesse which I left for him; the Morholt's spear and blood shed in his honour. He remembered how I made no avowal, but claimed a trial at arms, and the high nature of his heart has made him understand what men around him cannot; never can he know of the spell, yet he doubts and hopes and knows I have told no lie, and would have me prove my cause. Oh, but to win at arms by God's aid for him, and to enter his peace and to put on mail for him again. . . . But what am I thinking? He would take Iseult back: would I surrender her to him? . . . It would have been much better had he killed me in my sleep. For till now I was hunted and I could hate and forget; he had thrown Iseult to the lepers, she was no more his, but mine; and now by his compassion he has wakened my heart and regained the Queen. For Queen she was at his side, but in this wood she lives a slave, and I waste her youth; and for rooms all hung with silk she has this savage place, and a hut for her splendid walls, and I am the cause that she treads this ugly road. So now I cry to God the Lord, who is King of the world, and beg Him to give me strength to yield back Iseult to King Mark; for she is indeed his wife, wed according to the laws of Rome before all the barony of his land."

And as he thought thus, he leant upon his bow, and all through the night considered his sorrow.

Within the hollow of thorns that was their resting-place Iseult the Fair awaited Tristan's return. The golden ring that King Mark had slipped there glistened on her finger in the moonlight, and she thought:

"He that by the courtesy of his heart put on this ring is not the man who threw me to his lepers in his wrath; he is rather that compassionate lord who, from the day I touched his shore, received me and protected. And he loved Tristan once, but I came, and see what I have done! He should have lived in the King's palace amid an hundred squires who would have formed his suite and served him, to win their spurs; he should have ridden through King's and baron's fees, finding adventure; but through me he has forgotten his knighthood, and is hunted and exiled from the court leading a random life . . ."

Just then she heard the feet of Tristan coming over the dead leaves and twigs. She came to meet him, as was her wont, to relieve him of his arms, and she took from him his bow "Failnaught" and his arrows, and she unbuckled his sword-straps. And, "Friend," said he, "it is the King's sword. It should have slain, but it spared us."

Iseult took the sword, and kissed the hilt of gold, and Tristan saw her weeping.

"Friend," said he, "if I could make my peace with the King; if he would allow me to sustain in arms that neither by act nor word have I loved you with a wrongful love, any knight from the Marshes of Ely right away to Dureaume that would gainsay me, would find me armed in the ring. Then if the King would deign to keep me in his suite, I would serve him in all honour as my lord and my father; if he would keep you and drive me out I would cross to the Lowlands or to Brittany with Gorvenal alone. But wherever I went and always, Queen, I should be yours; nor would I have spoken thus, Iseult, but for the wretchedness you bear so long for my sake in this desert land."

"Tristan," she said, "there is the hermit Ogrin. Let us return to him, and cry mercy to the King of Heaven."

They wakened Gorvenal; Iseult mounted the steed, and Tristan led it by the bridle, and all night long they went for the last time through the woods of their love, and they did not speak a word. By morning they came to the hermitage, where Ogrin read at the threshold, and seeing them, called them tenderly:

"Friends," he cried, "see how Love drives you still to further wretchedness. Will you not do penance at last for your madness?"

"Lord Ogrin," said Tristan, "hear us. Help us to offer peace to the King, and I will yield him the Queen, and will myself go far away into Brittany or the Lowlands, and if someday the King suffer me, I will return and serve as I should."

And at the hermit's feet Iseult said in her turn:

"Nor will I live longer so, for though I will not say one word of penance for my love, which is there and remains forever, yet from now on I will be separate from him."

Then the hermit wept and praised God and cried: "High King, I praise Thy Name, for that Thou hast let me live so long as to give aid to these!"

And he gave them wise counsel, and took ink, and wrote a little writ offering the King what Tristan said. When he had written all, the latter sealed it with his ring.

"Who will bear this writ?" asked the hermit.

"I myself will bear it."

"No, Sir Tristan, you must not attempt this dangerous ride; I will go for you, I know the people of the castle well!"

"Give it me, fair master Ogrin; the Queen will remain in your hermitage; at nightfall I will go with my equerry, who will hold my horse."

As soon as darkness fell on the forest Tristan took the road with Gorvenal. At the gates of Tintagel he quit him. The sentinels on the walls sounded their bugles. He slipped into the moat and traversed the town at the peril of his life. As in other times he leaped over the sharp stakes of the orchard, saw again the marble round, the fountain and the tall pine-tree, and came beneath the window where the King slept. He called him gently, and Mark awoke and whispered:

"Who are you that call me in the night at such an hour?"

"Sire, I am Tristan: I bring you a writ, and lay it here on the grating of this window. Have your response hung to the arm of the Red Cross."

Then the King cried: "Nephew! Nephew! for God's sake wait awhile."

He ran to the sill and cried thrice into the night: "Tristan! Tristan! Tristan my son!" But Tristan had fled and joined his squire, and mounted rapidly. Gorvenal said to him:

"Oh, Tristan, you are mad to have come. Fly hard with me by the nearest road."

So they came back to the hermitage, and there they found Ogrin at prayer, but Iseult weeping silently.

THE

FORD

Mark had awakened his chaplain and had given him the writ to read; the chaplain broke the seal, saluted in Tristan's name, and then, when he had cunningly made out the written words, told him what Tristan offered; and Mark heard without saying a word, but his heart was glad, for he still loved the Queen.

He summoned by name the choicest of his baronage, and when they were all assembled they were silent and the King spoke:

"My lords, here is a writ, just sent me. I am your King, and you my lieges. Hear what is offered me, and then counsel me, for you owe me counsel."

The chaplain rose, unfolded the writ, and said, upstanding:

"My lords, it is Tristan that first sends love and homage to the King and all his barony, and he adds, 'O King, when I slew the dragon and conquered the King of Ireland's daughter it was to me they gave her. I was to ward her at will and I yielded her to you. Yet hardly had you wed her when felons made you accept their lies, and in your anger, fair uncle, my lord, you would have had us burnt without trial. But God took compassion on us; we prayed him and he saved the Queen, as justice was: and me also—though I leapt from a high rock, I was saved by the power of God. And since then what have I done blameworthy? The Queen was thrown to the lepers; I came to her succour and bore her away. Could I have done less for a woman, who all but died innocent through me? I fled through the woods. Nor could I have come down into the vale and yielded her, for there was a ban to take us dead or alive. But now, as then, I am ready, my lord, to sustain in arms against all comers that never had the Queen for me, nor I for her, a love dishonourable to you. Publish the lists, and if I cannot prove my right in arms, burn me before your men. But if I conquer and you take back Iseult, no baron of yours will serve you as will I; and if you will not have me, I will offer myself to the King of Galloway, or to him of the Lowlands, and you will hear of me never again. Take counsel, King, for if you will make no terms I will take back Iseult to Ireland, and she shall be Queen in her own land.' "

When the barons of Cornwall heard how Tristan offered battle, they said to the King:

"Sire, take back the Queen. They were madmen

that belied her to you. But as for Tristan, let him go and war it in Galloway, or in the Lowlands. Bid him bring back Iseult on such a day and that soon."

Then the King called thrice clearly:

"Will any man rise in accusation against Tristan?"

And as none replied, he said to his chaplain:

"Write me a writ in haste. You have heard what you shall write. Iseult has suffered enough in her youth. And let the writ be hung upon the arm of the Red Cross before evening. Write speedily." He added, "You will also say that I send them, both, greetings and love."

Towards midnight Tristan crossed the Heath of Sand, and found the writ, and bore it sealed to Ogrin; and the hermit read the letter; "How Mark consented by the counsel of his barons to take back Iseult, but not to keep Tristan for his liege. Rather let him cross the sea, when, on the third day hence, at the Ford of Chances, he had given back the Queen into King Mark's hands." Then Tristan said to the Queen:

"Oh, my God! I must lose you, friend! But it must be, since I can thus spare you what you suffer for my sake. But when we part for ever I will give you a pledge of mine to keep, and from whatever unknown land I reach I will send some messenger, and he will bring back word of you, and at your call I will come from far away."

Iseult said, sighing:

"Tristan, leave me your dog, Hodain, and every time I see him I will remember you, and will be less sad. And, friend, I have here a ring of green jasper. Take it for the love of me, and put it on your finger; then if anyone come saying he is from you, I will not trust him at all till he show me this ring, but once I have seen it, there is no power or royal ban that can prevent me from doing what you bid—wisdom or folly."

"Friend," he said, "here give I you Hodain."

"Friend," she replied, "take you this ring in reward."

And they kissed each other on the lips.

Now Ogrin, having left the lovers in the hermitage, hobbled upon his crutch to the place called The Mount, and he bought ermine there and fur and cloth of silk and purple and scarlet, and a palfrey harnessed in gold that went softly, and the folk laughed to see him spending upon these the small moneys he had amassed so long; but the old man put the rich stuffs upon the palfrey and came back to Iseult.

And "Queen," said he, "your raiment is in rags; take these gifts of mine that you may seem the finer on the day when you come to the Ford. I fear lest they displease you; I am not skilled in the selection of such things."

Meanwhile the King had had cried through Cornwall the news that on the third day he would make his peace with the Queen at the Ford, and knights and ladies came in a crowd to the gathering, for all loved the Queen and would see her, save the three felons that yet survived. But of these three, one will die by the sword, the other will perish pierced by an arrow, the third will drown; and, as for the woodman, Perinis the Loyal, the Fair will strike him to earth with blows of a club, in the woods. Thus God who hates all excess will avenge the lovers on their enemies.

On the day chosen for the meeting, the field shone

far with the rich tents of the barons. Through the forest Tristan rode with Iseult. In fear of an ambush he had worn his coat of mail beneath his rags. Suddenly Tristan and Iseult came out at the forest's edge, and caught sight of King Mark far off among his barony:

"Friend," said Tristan, "there is the King, your lord—his knights and his men; they are coming towards us, and very soon we may not speak to each other again. By the God of Power I conjure you, if ever I send you a word, do you my bidding."

"Friend," said Iseult, "on the day that I see the ring, nor tower, nor wall, nor stronghold will let me from doing the will of my friend."

"Why then," he said, "Iseult, may God reward you."

Their horses went abreast and he drew her towards him with his arm.

"Friend," said Iseult, "hear my last prayer: you will leave this land, but wait some days; hide till you know how the King may treat me, whether in wrath or kindness. I am alone: who will defend me from the felons? I am afraid. Friend, Orri the woodman will entertain you hidden. Go you by night to the abandoned cellar that you know and I will send Perinis there to say if anyone misuse me."

"Friend, none would dare. I will stay hidden with Orri, and if any misuse you let him fear me as the Enemy himself."

Now the two troops were near and they saluted, and the King rode a bow-shot before his men and with him Dinas of Lidan; and when the barons had come up, Tristan, holding Iseult's palfrey by the bridle, bowed to the King and said:

"O King, I yield you here Iseult the Fair, and I

summon you, before the men of your land, that I
may defend myself in your court, for I have had no
judgment. Let me have trial at arms, and if I am
conquered, burn me, but if I conquer keep me by
you, or, if you will not, I will be off to some far
country."

But no one took up Tristan's wager, and the
King, taking Iseult's palfrey by the bridle, gave it to
Dinas, and went apart to take counsel.

Dinas, in his joy, gave all honour and courtesy to
the Queen. He took her sumptuous mantle of scarlet
from her shoulders and her form gracefully emerged
in a fine tunic and great kirtle of silk. And the
Queen smiled, remembering the old hermit, who had
not spared his pence. Rich was her gown, delicate
her limbs, her eyes blue, her hair fair as the rays of
the sun.

But when the felons saw her so fair and honoured
as of old, they were stirred and rode to the King. At
the moment, a baron, André of Nicole, was striving to
persuade him: "Sire," he was saying, "keep Tristan
by you; thanks to him you will be a more dreaded
lord." And bit by bit he softened the heart of Mark.
But the felons opposed him and said:

"King, hear our counsel. That the Queen was slan-
dered we admit, but if she and Tristan re-enter your
court together, rumour will revive again. Rather let
Tristan go apart awhile. Doubtless some day you
may recall him."

And so Mark did, and ordered Tristan by his
barons to go off without delay.

Then Tristan came near the Queen for his farewell, and as they looked at one another the Queen in
shame of that assembly blushed, but the King pitied
her, and spoke his nephew thus for the first time:

"You cannot leave in these rags; take then from my treasury gold and silver and white fur and grey, as much as you will."

"King," said Tristan, "neither a penny nor a link of mail. I will go as I can, and serve with high heart the mighty King in the Lowlands."

And he turned rein and went down towards the sea, but Iseult followed him with her eyes and so long as he could yet be seen a long way off she did not turn.

Now at the news of the peace, men, women and children, great and small, ran out of the town in a crowd to meet Iseult, and while they mourned Tristan's exile they rejoiced at the Queen's return.

And to the noise of bells, and over pavings strewn with branches, the King and his counts and princes made her escort, and the gates of the palace were thrown open that rich and poor might enter and eat and drink at will.

And Mark freed a hundred of his slaves, and armed a score of squires that day with hauberk and with sword.

But Tristan that night hid with Orri, as the Queen had counselled him. Let the felons beware!

THE

ORDEAL

BY

IRON

Dcnoalen, Andret, and Gondoïne held themselves safe; Tristan was far over sea, far away in service of a distant king, and they beyond his power. Therefore, during a hunt one day, as the King rode apart in a glade where the pack would pass, and hearkening to the hounds, they all three rode towards him, and said:

"O King, we have somewhat to say. Once you condemned the Queen without judgment and that was wrong; now you acquit her without judgment and that is wrong. She is not quit by trial, and the barons of your land blame you both. Counsel her, then, to claim the ordeal in God's judgment, for since she is innocent, she may swear on the relics of the saints that she has never erred, and hot iron will not hurt her. For so custom runs, and in this easy way are doubts dissolved."

But Mark answered:

"God strike you, my Cornish lords, how you hunt my shame! For you have I exiled my nephew, and now what would you now? Would you have me drive the Queen to Ireland too? What novel plaints have you to plead? Did not Tristan offer you battle in this matter? He offered battle to clear the Queen forever: he offered and you heard him all. Where then were your lances and your shields? My lords, your demands are unrighteous; beware lest I call back the man I exiled for your sakes!"

The dastards trembled; already they saw Tristan returned and bleeding their bodies white.

"Sire," they said, "we have counselled you loyal counsel as lieges and to your honour; henceforward we hold our peace. Put aside your anger and give us your safeguard."

But Mark stood up in the stirrup and cried:

"Out of my land, and out of my peace, all of you! Tristan I exiled for you, and now go you in turn, out of my land!"

But they answered:

"Sire, it is well. Our keeps are strong and fenced, and stand on rocks not easy for men to climb."

And they rode off without a salutation.

But the King (not tarrying for huntsman or for hound but straight away) spurred his horse to Tintagel; and as he sprang up the stairs the Queen heard the jangle of his spurs upon the stones.

She rose to meet him, and took his sword as she was wont, and bowed before him, as it was also her wont to do; but Mark raised her, holding her hands; and when Iseult looked up she saw his noble face in just that wrath she had seen before the faggot fire.

She thought that Tristan was found, and her heart grew cold, and without a word she fell at the King's feet.

He took her in his arms and kissed her gently till she could speak again, and then he said:

"Friend, friend, what evil tries you?"

"Sire, I am afraid, for I have seen your anger."

"Yes, I was angered at the hunt."

"My lord, should one take so deeply the mischances of a game?"

Mark smiled and said:

"No, friend; no chance of hunting vexed me, but those three felons who long have hated us. You know them: Andret, Denoalen and Gondoïne. I have driven them forth from my land."

"Sire, what did they say, or dare to say of me?"

"What matter? I have driven them forth."

"Sire, all living have this right: to say the word they have conceived. But I also have the right to know the fault of which I am accused. And from whom can I hear it, beside yourself? I am alone in a foreign land, and have no one else to defend me."

"They would have it that you should quit yourself by solemn oath and by the ordeal of iron, saying 'that God was a true judge, and that as the Queen was innocent, she herself should seek such judgment as would clear her for ever. These ordeals are without terror for him who knows himself innocent. How can they harm him? God is a true judge; he will for ever dissipate the old grievances.' This was their clamour and their demand incessantly. But let us leave it. I tell you, I have driven them forth."

Iseult trembled, but looking straight at the King, she said:

"Sire, call them back; I will clear myself by oath."

"When?"

"Ten days hence."

"Friend, this date is very near."

"It is only too distant. But I bargain this: that on the appointed day you call King Arthur and Lord Gawain, Girflet, Kay the seneschal, and a hundred of his knights to ride to the Sandy Heath where your land marches with his, and a river flows between; for I will not swear before your barons alone, lest they should demand some new thing, and lest there should be no end to my trials. But if my warrantors, King Arthur and his knights, be there, the barons will not dare dispute the judgment."

But as the heralds rode to Carduel, Iseult sent to Tristan secretly her squire Perinis: and he ran through the underwood, avoiding paths, till he found the hut of Orri, the woodman, where Tristan for many days had awaited news. Perinis told him all: the ordeal, the place and the time, and added:

"My lord, the Queen would have you on that day and place come dressed as a pilgrim, so that none may know you—unarmed, so that none may challenge—to the Sandy Heath. She must cross the river to the place appointed in a skiff. Beyond it, where Arthur and his hundred knights will stand, be you also. Doubtless you will be able to help her, there. My lady dreads the day of judgment: nevertheless she trusts in the courtesy of God, who once before saved her from the hands of the lepers."

Then Tristan answered:

"Go back, friend Perinis, return you to the Queen, and say that I will do her bidding."

And you must know that as Perinis went back to Tintagel he caught sight of that same woodman who had betrayed the lovers before, and the woodman, as he found him, had just dug a pitfall for wolves and for wild boars, and covered it with leafy branches to hide it, and as Perinis came near the woodman fled, but Perinis drove him, and caught him, at the pit's mouth.

"Spy, who sold the Queen, why run? Stay here near your grave which you yourself have troubled to dig."

His staff whirled in the air and hummed. And staff and skull broke at one time, and Perinis the Fair, the Faithful thrust the corpse with his feet into the branch-covered pitfall.

On the appointed day King Mark and Iseult, and the barons of Cornwall, having ridden as far as White-Lands, arrived in fine array at the river, and massed on the other share, the hosts of Arthur bowed their brilliant standards to them.

And just before them, sitting on the shore, was a poor pilgrim, wrapped in cloak and hood, who held his wooden platter and begged alms, in piercing, mournful tones.

Now as the Cornish boats came to the shoal of the further bank, Iseult said to the knights:

"My lords, how shall I land without befouling my clothes in the river-mud? Fetch me a ferryman."

And one of the knights hailed the pilgrim, and said:

"Friend, truss your coat, and try the water; carry you the Queen to shore, unless you fear the burden."

But as he took the Queen in his arms she whispered to him:

"Friend."

And then she whispered to him, lower still:

"Stumble you upon the sand."

And as he touched shore, he stumbled, holding the Queen in his arms; and the squires and boatmen with their oars and boat-hooks drove the poor pilgrim away.

But the Queen said:

"Let him be; some great travail and journey has weakened him."

And she threw to the pilgrim a little clasp of gold.

Before the tent of King Arthur was spread a rich Nicean cloth upon the grass, and the holy relics were set on it, taken out of their covers and their shrines.

And round the holy relics on the sward stood a guard more than a king's guard, for Lord Gawain, Girflet, and Kay the seneschal kept ward over them.

The Queen having prayed God, took off the jewels from her neck and hands, and gave them to the beggars around; she took off her purple mantle, and her overdress, and her shoes with their precious stones, and gave them also to the poor that loved her.

She kept upon her only the sleeveless tunic, and then with arms and feet quite bare she came between the two Kings, and all around the barons watched her in silence, and some wept, for near the holy relics was a brazier burning.

And trembling a little she stretched her right hand towards the bones and said: "Kings of Logres and of Cornwall; my lords Gawain, and Kay and Girflet, and all of you that are my warrantors, by these holy things and all the holy things of earth, I swear that no man born of woman has held me in his arms saving King Mark, my lord, and that poor pilgrim who only now took a fall, as you saw. King Mark, will that oath stand?"

"Yes, Queen," he said, "and God see to it."

"Amen," said Iseult, and then she went near the brazier, pale and stumbling, and all were silent. The iron was red, but she thrust her bare arms among the coals and seized it, and bearing it took nine steps.

Then, as she cast it from her, she stretched her arms out in a cross, with the palms of her hands wide open, and all men saw them fresh and clean and cold. Seeing that great sight the Kings and the barons and the people stood for a moment silent, then they stirred together and they praised God loudly all around.

THE

VOICE

OF

THE

NIGHTINGALE

When Tristan had come back to Orri's hut, and had loosened his heavy pilgrim's cape, he saw clearly in his heart that it was time to keep his oath to King Mark and to fly the land.

Why did he tarry? The Queen had cleared herself, the King cherished and honoured her. Arthur if needs be would take her under his protection, and besides, no felony could prevail against her. Why longer prowl about the environs of Tintagel? It was but vainly to risk his own life and the life of the woodman and Iseult's tranquillity. Yes, he was leaving, and it had been for the last time, in his pilgrim's gown at White-Lands, that he had felt Iseult's fair body trembling in his arms.

Three days yet he tarried, because he could not drag himself away from that earth, but on the fourth day he thanked the woodman, and said to Gorvenal:

"Master, the hour of long separation has come; we are going to the land of Wales."

They took the road sadly by night. But their way skirted the orchard-close where not long since Tristan used to await his friend. The night shone, clear. At a turn of the road, not far from the palings, he saw rising in the brightness, the robust trunk of the tall pine-tree.

"Good master, wait under these nearby trees; I will not be long."

"Where are you going? Madman, will you for ever be seeking death?"

But already with a light bound Tristan had o'er-leaped the palisade of stakes. He went to the tall pine near the bright marble round. What use now, throwing wood-shavings into the spring? Iseult would not come again. With supple, careful steps he ventured along the path which the Queen used to take, towards the castle.

In her chamber Iseult lay sleepless in the arms of the sleeping Mark. Suddenly, through the open window where the moonbeams moved, came the voice of a nightingale. Iseult listened to the loud bird-throat that charmed the night, and the tones rose plaintively and such that there exists no cruel heart, no murderer's heart, that would not have been touched. The Queen wondered: "Whence comes this melody?" Suddenly she understood: "It is Tristan! Thus in the wood of Morois he used to imitate song-birds for my delight. He is leaving; this is his last adieu. How he laments, like the nightingale when he takes leave, at summer's end, in very sadness. Friend, never again will I hear your voice!"

The melody quivered with fervour.

"Ah, what do you ask? That I come? No. Remember Ogrin the hermit, and the oaths sworn by me. Be still, death waits for us. . . . What does death matter? You call me, you want me, I come!"

She slipped from the King's arms and threw a mantle lined with grey wool about her almost unclothed body. She had to traverse the adjoining hall where each night ten knights kept watch turn by turn: while five of them slept, the other five stood fully armed, alert at the doors and windows. But by luck they were all asleep, five on the beds, five on the flagstones. Iseult stepped over their scattered forms, lifted the bar of the great door: the metal sounded, but without wakening any of the watch. She stepped over the sill. And the songster grew silent.

Under the trees, without a word, he pressed her to his breast; their arms closed firmly about each other's bodies, and till dawn, as though tied with cords, they did not break from the embrace. Despite Mark and the watch, the lovers took their bliss.

The night under the trees maddened the lovers; and on the following days, Mark having quit Tintagel to hold his sittings at St. Lubin, Tristan who had returned to Orri's hut, boldly slipped every morning in broad daylight through the orchard to the women's quarters.

A serf spied him and went to Andret, Denoalen and Gondoïne:

"My lords, the beast whom you thought to have turned out has returned to the lair."

"Who?"

"Tristan."

"When did you see him?"

"This morning, and I knew him well. And to-morrow at dawn you likewise can see him coming, girt with a sword, a bow in one hand, two arrows in the other."

"Where can we see him?"

"From a certain window which I know. But if J show him to you, how much will you give me?"

"A silver mark, and you will be a wealthy boor."

"Listen then," said the serf. "One can see into the Queen's chamber from a narrow window which commands it, for it is pierced very high in the wall. But a great curtain stretched across the room masks the opening. To-morrow let one of you boldly enter the orchard, cut a long thorn-branch and sharpen it at the end; let him lift himself to the high window and stick the branch like a fork into the stuff of the curtain; thus he can easily divide it, and you can have me burned, my lords, if behind the hangings you do not see what I have told you."

Andret, Gondoïne and Denoalen argued amongst themselves which of them was first to have the joy of the sight, and decided at length to concede it first to Gondoïne. Each went his way: To-morrow at dawn they were to meet. To-morrow, at dawn, noble lords, beware of Tristan!

On the morrow, while the night still was dark, Tristan, quitting the hut of Orri the woodman, crept towards the castle through thickets of thorn-bushes. Leaving a copse he looked through a clearing and saw Gondoïne coming from his manor. He dropped behind the thorns and placed himself in ambush:

"Ah, God, grant that he who is approaching down there will not see me till the right instant!"

Sword in hand, he waited; but by chance Gondoïne took another path and moved off. Tristan disappointed came forth, drew his bow, took aim; alas, the man was already out of range.

At this moment, behold coming from afar, softly descending the path at the ambling pace of a small black palfrey, Denoalen, followed by two great hounds. Tristan awaited him, concealed behind an apple-tree. He saw him rousing his dogs to start a stag in a coppice. But before the hounds shall have driven *him* from his lair, their master will have received a wound of a sort that no physician can cure. As soon as Denoalen was close to him, Tristan threw his cape, sprang forth and stood before his foe. The traitor sought to fly; in vain; he had not time to cry "You have wounded me!" He fell from his horse. Tristan cut off his head, cut off the braids that hung about his face and put them in his hose, wishing to show them to Iseult and therewith gladden his friend's heart. "Alas," thought he, "what has become of Gondoïne? He has escaped: why could I not pay him a like wage?"

He wiped his sword, placed it in its scabbard, dragged a tree-trunk onto the corpse, and leaving the pool of blood, hastened away, his hood on his head, towards his friend.

Gondoïne had outstripped him: already at Tintagel, at the high window, he had stuck his thorn-stick into the curtain, lightly divided two sections of the fabric, and was peering into the rush-strewn chamber. At first he saw no one save Perinis; then Brangien, still holding the comb with which she had been combing the Queen with the golden hair. But Iseult entered, then Tristan. In one hand he carried his willow-wood bow and two arrows; in the other he

held two long braids of man's hair. He let his cape
fall and his fine figure stood plain. Iseult the Fair
bowed to greet him, and as she drew herself up and
raised her face towards him, she saw, cast on the
hangings, the shadow of Gondoïne's head. Tristan
said:

"See you these fine braids? They belong to Denoalen. I have avenged you on him. Never more will he
buy or sell shield or lance!"

"That is well, my lord: but draw this bow, I pray
you; I want to see whether it stretches readily."

Tristan drew, astounded, half understanding.

Iseult took one of the arrows, fitted it, looked to
see that the string was secure, and in a low, rapid
voice said:

"I see something that offends me. Aim well, Tristan!"

He took his stance, raised his head and saw, high
on the curtain, the shadow of Gondoïne's head.
"May God," said he, "direct this arrow!" So saying,
he faced the wall and drew. The long arrow whistled
through the air, swifter than merlin or swallow, split
the dastard's eye, cut his brain like an apple's flesh
and, pulsing, stuck in his skull. Without a cry
Gondoïne crashed down and fell atop a fence stake.

Iseult then said to Tristan:

"Fly now, friend! You see, the felons know your
hiding-place. Andret still lives, he will inform the
King; you are no longer safe in the woodman's hut.
Fly, friend! Perinis the Faithful will conceal the
body in the woods so well that the King will never
learn of this. But you, fly from this land, for your
safety, for mine!"

Tristan said:

"How can I live?"

"Yes, friend Tristan, our lives are entwined and interwoven one with the other. And I, how can I live? My body remains here, you have my heart."

"Iseult, my friend, I go, I know not to what land. But if ever you see the ring of green jasper, will you do what I bid you through it?"

"Yes, you know that: if ever I see the green jasper ring again, neither tower, nor stronghold, nor royal prohibition, will keep me from doing the will of my friend, be it folly or wisdom."

"Friend, may the God born in Bethlehem reward you for it!"

"Friend, may God keep you!"

THE

LITTLE

FAIRY

BELL

Tristan took refuge in Wales, in the land of the great Duke Gilain, who was young, powerful and frank in spirit, and welcomed him nobly as a god-sent guest.

And he did everything to give him honour and joy; but he found that neither adventure, nor feast could soothe what Tristan suffered.

One day, as he sat by the young Duke's side his spirit weighed upon him so that not knowing it he groaned, and the Duke, to soothe him, ordered into his private room his favourite toy, a fairy thing, which pleased his eyes when he was sad and relieved his own heart; on a table covered with rich, good purple, valets placed his dog Pticru. This dog was a magic dog; it had come to the Duke from the isle of Avalon. A fairy had given it him as a love-gift, and no one can well describe its kind or beauty. Its hide was coloured with tints so marvellously distributed that one could not say of what colour it was: its neck at first appearance seemed whiter than snow, its rump greener than a clover-leaf, one of the flanks the red of scarlet, the other yellow like saffron, the belly blue like lapis-lazuli, the back rosy; but if one looked a long while, all these colours danced before the eye, changed, became in turn white and green, yellow, blue, purplish, dark or clear. At the neck, hung by a chain of gold, it bore a little bell; and that tinkled so gaily, and so clear and so soft, that as Tristan heard it, he was soothed, and his anguish melted away, and he forgot all that he had suffered for the Queen; for such was the virtue of the bell and such its property: that whosoever heard it, he lost all pain. And as Tristan stroked the little fairy thing, the dog that took away his sorrow, he saw how delicate it was and fine, and how it had soft hair like samite, and he thought how good a gift it would make for the Queen. But he dared not ask for it right out since he knew that the Duke loved this dog beyond everything in the world, and would yield it to no prayers, nor to wealth, nor to wile; so one day Tristan having made a plan in his mind said this:

"Lord, what would you give to the man who could rid your land of the hairy giant Urgan, that levies such a toll?"

"Truly, the victor might choose what he would, but none will dare."

Then said Tristan:

"Those are strange words, for good comes to no land save by risk and daring, and not for all the gold of Milan would I renounce my desire to fight him in his wood and bring him down."

"Then," said Duke Gilain, "may the God born of a Virgin be with you and preserve you from death."

Then Tristan went out to find Urgan in his lair, and they fought hard and long, till courage conquered strength, and Tristan, having cut off the giant's hand, bore it back to the Duke.

And "Sire," said he, "since I may choose a reward according to your word, give me Pticru, your little fairy dog."

"Friend, what have you asked? Leave it me and take rather my sister and the half of my land."

"Sire, your sister is fair and fair is your land; but it was to win your fairy dog that I attacked Urgan the Hairy. Remember your promise!"

"Friend," said the Duke, "take it, then, but in taking it you take away also all my joy."

Then Tristan took the little fairy dog and gave it in ward to a Welsh harper, who was cunning and who bore it to Cornwall till he came to Tintagel, and having come there put it secretly into Brangien's hands, and the Queen was so pleased that she gave ten marks of gold to the harper, but she put it about that the Queen of Ireland, her mother, had sent the beast. And she had a goldsmith work a little kennel for him, all jewelled, and incrusted with gold and enamel inlaid; and wherever she went she carried the dog with her in memory of her friend, and as she watched it sadness and anguish and regrets melted out of her heart.

At first she did not guess the marvel, but thought her consolation was because the gift was Tristan's, till one day she found that it was fairy, and that it was the little bell that charmed her soul; then she thought: "What have I to do with comfort since he is sorrowing? He could have kept it too and have forgotten his sorrow; but with high courtesy he sent it me to give me his joy and to take up his pain again. But it is unbecoming that things should be thus; Tristan, while you suffer, so long will I suffer also."

And she took the magic bell and shook it just a little, and then by the open window she threw it into the sea.

ISEULT

OF

THE

WHITE

HANDS

Apart the lovers could neither live nor die, for it was life and death together; and Tristan fled his sorrow through seas and islands and many lands.

He fled his sorrow still by seas and islands, till at last he came back to his land of Lyonesse and there Rohalt, the Keeper of Faith, welcomed him with happy tears and called him son. But he could not live in the peace of his own land, and he turned again and rode through kingdoms and through baronies, seeking adventure. From the Lyonesse to the Lowlands, from the Lowlands on to the Germanies;

through the Germanies and into Spain. And many
lords he served, and many deeds did, but for two
years no news came to him out of Cornwall, nor
friend, nor messenger. Then he thought that Iseult
had forgotten.

Now it happened one day that, riding with Gorvenal alone, he came into the land of Brittany. They
rode through a wasted plain of ruined walls and
empty hamlets and burnt fields everywhere, and the
earth deserted of men; and Tristan thought:

"I am weary, and my deeds profit me nothing; my
lady is far off and I shall never see her again. Or
why for two years has she made no sign, or why has
she sent no messenger to find me as I wandered? But
in Tintagel Mark honours her and she gives him joy,
and that little fairy bell has done a thorough work;
for little she remembers or cares for the joys and the
mourning of old, little for me, as I wander in this
desert place. I in my turn, shall I never forget her
who forgets me? Will I never find someone to heal
me of my unhappiness?"

During two days Tristan and Gorvenal passed
fields and towns without seeing man, cock or dog.
On the third day, at the hour of noon, they came
near a hill where an old chantry stood and close by a
hermitage also. The hermit wore no woven habit on
his back, but a goat-skin and some rags of linen.
Prostrate on the ground he prayed Mary Magdalen
to inspire him with salutary prayers. He bade the
wayfarers welcome, and while Gorvenal stabled the
horses, helped Tristan disarm, then laid out the
food. He did not give them delicate viands, but
spring-water and barley-bread baked in ashes. After
the meal, the night having fallen and they having

seated themselves about the fire, Tristan asked what wasted land that was, and the hermit answered:

"Lord, it is Breton land which Duke Hoël holds, and once it was rich in pasture and ploughland, with mills here, apple-orchards there, and many small farms. But Count Riol of Nantes has wasted it. His pillagers have set fires everywhere and everywhere taken booty. His men will be rich a long while; but that is war."

"Brother," said Tristan, "why does Count Riol thus dishonour your lord, Hoël?"

"My lord, I will tell you the cause of this war. Know that this Count Riol was the Duke's vassal. And the Duke has a daughter, fair among all King's daughters, and Count Riol would have taken her to wife; but her father refused her to a vassal, and Count Riol would have carried her away by force. Many men have died in that quarrel."

And Tristan asked:

"Can the Duke continue to wage this war?"

And the hermit answered:

"Hardly, my lord; yet his last keep of Carhaix holds out still, for the walls are strong, and strong is the heart of the Duke's son Kaherdin, a very good knight and bold; but the enemy surrounds them on every side and starves them. Very hardly do they hold their castle."

Then Tristan asked:

"How far is this keep of Carhaix?"

"Sir," said the hermit, "it is but two miles further on this way."

Then Tristan and Gorvenal lay down, for it was evening.

In the morning, when they had slept, and when

the hermit had chanted, and had shared his black bread with them, Tristan thanked him and rode hard to Carhaix. And as he halted beneath the fast high walls, he saw a little company of men behind the battlements, and he asked if the Duke were there with his son Kaherdin. Now Hoël was among them; and when he cried "yes," Tristan called up to him and said:

"I am that Tristan, King of Lyonesse, and Mark of Cornwall is my uncle. I have heard that your vassals do you a wrong, and I have come to offer you my arms."

"Alas, Lord Tristan, go you your way alone and God reward you, for here within we have no more food; no wheat, or meat, or any stores but only lentils and a little oats remaining."

But Tristan said:

"For two years I dwelt in a forest, eating nothing save roots and herbs and venison; yet I found it a good life, so open you the door."

Kaherdin then said:

"Take him in, my father, since he is so brave, that he may share our fortunes and misfortunes."

They welcomed him with honour, and Kaherdin showed him the walls and the dungeon keep with all their devices, and from the battlements he showed the plain where far away gleamed the tents of Count Riol. And when they were down in the castle again he said to Tristan:

"Friend, let us go the the hall where my mother and sister sit."

So, holding each other's hands, they came into the women's room, where the mother and the daughter sat together weaving gold upon English cloth and singing a weaving song. They sang of Doette the fair who sits alone beneath the white-thorn, and round about her blows the wind. She waits for Doon, her friend, but he tarries long and does not come. This was the song they sang. And Tristan bowed to them, and they to him. Then Kaherdin, showing the work his mother did, said:

"See, friend Tristan, what a work-woman is here, and how marvellously she adorns stoles and chasubles for the poor ministers, and how my sister's hands run thread of gold upon this cloth. Of right, good sister, are you called 'Iseult of the White Hands.' "

But Tristan, hearing her name, smiled and looked at her more gently.

Now, Count Riol had pitched his camp three miles from Carhaix, and since many days Duke Hoël's men had not dared go beyond the barriers to assail him. But on the morrow, Tristan, Kaherdin, and twelve young knights left the castle and rode to a pine-wood near the enemy's tents. And sprang from ambush and captured a wagon of Count Riol's food; and from that day, by escapade and ruse they would carry tents and convoys and kill off men, nor ever come back without some booty; so that Tristan and Kaherdin began to be brothers in arms, and kept faith and tenderness, as history tells. And as they came back from these rides, talking chivalry together, often did Kaherdin praise to his comrade his sister, Iseult of the White Hands, for her simplicity and beauty.

One day, as the dawn broke, a sentinel ran from the tower through the halls crying:

"Lords, you have slept too long; rise, for an assault is on."

And knights and burgesses armed, and ran to the

walls, and saw helmets shining on the plain, and
pennons streaming crimson, like flames, and all the
host of Riol in its array. Then the Duke and Kaherdin deployed their horsemen before the gates, and
from a bow-length off they stooped, and spurred and
charged, and they put their lances down together
and the arrows fell on them like April rain.

Now Tristan had armed himself among the last of
those the sentinel had roused, and he laced his shoes
of steel, and put on his mail, and his spurs of gold,
his hauberk, and his helm over the gorget, and he
mounted and spurred, with shield on breast, crying:
"Carhaix!"

It was high time: Hoël's men already were falling
back towards the gates. Then it was a sight to see,
the mêlée of overthrown horses and wounded
vassals, the blows dealt by the young knights, and
the grass that underfoot grew bloody. In front of all,
Kaherdin proudly had stopped, to meet the charge
of a brave baron, the brother of Count Riol. They
crashed with lowered lances. That of the man of
Nantes broke off without unseating Kaherdin who
with a skilful blow split his adversary's shield and
plunged his polished steel up to the pennant into his
side. Lifted from his saddle, the knight, unhorsed,
fell to the ground. At the cry his brother gave, Count
Riol came charging, rein free, at Kaherdin, but Tristan came in between. So they met, Tristan and
Count Riol. And at the shock Tristan's lance shivered, but Riol's lance struck Tristan's horse just
where the breast-piece runs, and laid it on the field.

But Tristan, standing, drew his sword, his bur-
nished sword, and said:

"Coward! Here is death ready for the man that
strikes the horse before the rider."

But Riol answered:

"I think you have lied, my lord!"

And he charged him.

And as he passed, Tristan let fall his sword so heavily upon his helm that he carried away the crest and the nasal, but the sword slipped on the mailed shoulder, and glanced on the horse, and killed it, so that of force Count Riol must slip the stirrup and leap and feel the ground. Then Riol too was on his feet, and they both fought hard in their broken mail, their 'scutcheons torn and their helmets loosened and lashing with their dented swords, till Tristan struck Riol just where the helmet buckles, and it yielded and the blow was struck so hard that the baron fell on hands and knees.

"Rise if you can, vassal," cried Tristan to him. "It was an evil hour that you came into this field; you must die." Riol regained his stand, but Tristan struck him down once more with a blow that split the helm, and it split the headpiece too, and touched the skull; then Riol cried mercy and begged his life, and Tristan took his sword.

It was just in time, for from all sides the men of Nantes were charging to the rescue of their lord. But already their lord had surrendered.

So he promised to enter Duke Hoël's keep and to swear homage again, and to restore what he had wasted; and by his order the battle ceased, and his host went off discomfited.

Now when the victors were returned Kaherdin said to his father:

"Sire, keep you Tristan. There is no better knight, and your land has need of such courage."

So when the Duke had taken counsel with his barons, he said to Tristan:

"Friend, you have won my love, for I owe you my land, but I shall be quit with you if you will take my daughter, Iseult of the White Hands, who comes of kings and of queens, and of dukes before them in blood. Take her, she is yours."

And Tristan answered:

"I will take her, Sire."

Ah, my lords, why did he speak that word? That word cost him his life.

So the day was fixed, and the Duke came with his friends and Tristan with his, and before all, at the gate of the minster, Tristan wed Iseult of the White Hands, according to the Church's law.

But that same night, as Tristan's valets undressed him, it happened that in drawing his arm from the sleeve they drew off and let fall from his finger the ring of green jasper, the ring of Iseult the Fair. It sounded on the stones, and Tristan looked and saw it. Then his heart awoke and he knew that he had done wrong. For he remembered the day when Iseult the Fair had given him the ring. It was in that forest where, for his sake, she had led the hard life with him, and that night he saw again the hut in the wood of Morois, and he was bitter with himself that ever he had accused her of treason; for now it was he that had betrayed, and he was bitter with himself also in pity for this new wife and her simplicity and beauty. See how these two Iseults had met him in an evil hour, and to both had he broken faith!

Now Iseult of the White Hands wondered to hear him sigh, lying at her side. A little shamed she said at last:

"Dear lord, have I hurt you in anything? Why do you not give me even a single kiss? Tell me the manner, that I may know my fault, and I will make all amends that I can."

But Tristan answered: "Friend, do not be angry with me; for once in another land I fought a foul dragon and was near to death, and I thought of the Mother of God, and I made a vow to Her that, delivered from the dragon through Her courtesy, would I ever wed, for one year I would abstain from embracing and kissing my wife."

"Since that is so," said Iseult, "I will gladly endure it."

But when in the morning the servants put the wimple of the married woman on her, she smiled sadly and thought how little right she had to this head-dress.

KAHERDIN

Several days afterward, Duke Hoël, his seneschal, his huntsmen, Tristan, Iseult of the White Hands and Kaherdin together left the castle to hunt in the forest. On a narrow path Tristan rode to the left of Kaherdin who with his right hand led by the rein the palfrey of Iseult of the White Hands. Now the palfrey stumbled in a puddle of water. Its hoof splashed water so rudely under Iseult's clothing that she was drenched and felt coldness above her knee. She gave a light cry and spurring her horse forward laughed so loudly and clearly that Kaherdin, galloping after her and having caught up with her, asked:

"Fair sister, why do you laugh?"

"It was a thought which came to me, fair brother. When that water splashed me, I said to it, 'Water, you are bolder than ever was the bold Sir Tristan.' That was why I laughed. But I have already said too much, brother, and repent me." Astonished, Kaherdin entreated her so keenly that at length she told him the truth about her marriage.

Tristan caught up with them and all three rode in silence as far as the hunting-lodge. There, Kaherdin called Tristan aside and said to him:

"Sir Tristan, my sister has confessed the truth about her marriage to me. I took you for my peer, and as my comrade. But you have betrayed your faith and shamed our family. From this time forth, if you do not give me satisfaction, know that I challenge you."

Tristan answered him:

"It is true, I have come among you to your misfortune. But learn of my unhappiness, fair sweet friend, brother and comrade, and perhaps your heart will be appeased. Know that I have another Iseult, fairest of all women, who for my sake has suffered and still suffers many a pang. Of a truth, your sister loves me and does me honour, yet for the love of me the other Iseult treats, with even more honour than your sister treats me, a dog which I gave her. Come, let us quit this hunt; follow where I shall take you; I will tell you of my misery."

Tristan turned his horse's head and gave spur. Kaherdin galloped after him. Without speaking they rode into the forest depths. There Tristan laid bare his life to Kaherdin. He told him how, on the high sea, he had drunk love and death; about the treachery of the barons and the dwarf; of the Queen led to the stake, delivered to the lepers, and of their loves in the wild forest; how he had given her back to Mark, and having fled her, had wished to love Iseult of the White Hands; and how he now knew that he could neither live nor die without the Queen. Kaherdin was silent and astounded. He felt his anger sinking against his will.

"Friend," he finally said, "I hear wondrous words and you have moved my heart to pity, for you have endured pangs from which God save one and all of us! Let us go back to Carhaix: three days hence, if I can, I will tell you my mind."

Within her room at Tintagel, Iseult the Fair sighed for the sake of Tristan, calling him in her heart. To love him always, she had no other thought, no other hope, no other wish. All her desire was in him, and for two years now she had not heard from him. Where was he? In what country? Was he even alive?

Within her room at Tintagel Iseult the Fair sat singing a song she had made. She sang of Guron taken and killed for his love, and how by guile the count gave Guron's heart to her to eat, and of her woe. The Queen sang softly, catching the harp's tone; her hands were cunning and her song good; she sang low down and softly.

Then came in Kariado, a rich count from a far off island that had fared to Tintagel to offer the Queen his service, and several times since Tristan's leaving he had sought her in love. But the Queen repelled his advances, calling them folly. He was a comely knight, vain, proud, eloquent, but a hero oftener in the chambers of the women than in battle. He found Iseult as she sang and laughed to her:

"Lady, how sad a song! as sad as the osprey's; do they not say he sings for death? and your song means that to me; I die for you."

And Iseult said: "So let it be and may it mean so; for never come you here but to stir in me anger or mourning. Ever were you the screech owl or the osprey that boded ill when you spoke of Tristan; what news bear you now?"

And Kariado answered:

"You are angered, I know not why, but who heeds your words? Let the osprey bode me death; here is the evil news the screech owl brings. Lady Iseult, Tristan, your friend, is lost to you. He has wed in a far land. So seek you other where, for he mocks your love. He has wed in great pomp Iseult of the White Hands, the King of Brittany's daughter."

And Kariado went off in anger, but Iseult bowed her head and broke into tears.

On the third day, Kaherdin called Tristan:

"Friend, I have taken counsel in my heart. Yes, you have told me the truth, the life you live in this land is frenzy and madness, and no good can come of it for either you or my sister Iseult of the White Hands. Hear what I propose. We will travel together to Tintagel; you will see the Queen and learn whether she still regrets you and is faithful to you. If she has forgotten you, then perhaps you will hold in greater fondness my sister Iseult, the Fair, the Simple. I will follow you: am I not your peer and your comrade?"

"Brother," said Tristan, "well has it been spoken 'The heart of a man is worth all the gold in a country.'"

Soon after Tristan and Kaherdin donned the cords and cowls of pilgrims, as though they intended to visit the graves of saints in distant lands. They said farewell to Duke Hoël. Tristan took Gorvenal, and Kaherdin a single equerry. Secretly they fitted out a ship and all four sailed towards Cornwall. The wind was light and favourable to them, so that they landed one morning before daybreak not far from Tintagel, in a lonely cove close by the castle of Lidan. There doubtless Dinas of Lidan the good seneschal would receive them and conceal their coming.

At daybreak the four companions were climbing towards Lidan when they spied coming behind them a man travelling their road at the slow gait of his horse. They took cover and the man passed without seeing them, for he slumbered in his saddle. Tristan recognized him:

"Brother," he whispered to Kaherdin, "it is Dinas of Lidan himself. He is asleep. Without doubt he is returning from his friend's house and still dreams of her: it would not be courteous to awake him, but follow me at a distance."

He rejoined Dinas, softly took his horse by the bridle and walked noiselessly by his side. At last a misstep of the horse awakened the sleeper. He opened his eyes, saw Tristan, hesitated:

"It's you, it's you, Tristan! God bless the hour in which I see you again: I have long awaited it!"

"Friend, God keep you! What news can you give me of the Queen?" "Harsh news, alas. The King loves her and would have her happy, but since your exile she languishes and weeps for you. But why go back to her? You do not seek your death and hers? Tristan, have mercy on the Queen, leave her be!"

"Do me this favour, friend," said Tristan. "Hide me at Lidan, take her my message, and bring it about that I see her once again, one single time!"

"I am sorry for my lady," Dinas responded, "and I will not take your message unless I know that she has remained dearer to you than all other women."

"My lord, you can tell her that she has remained dearer to me than all other women, and it will be the truth."

"Well then, follow me, Tristan; I will help you in your design."

At Lidan the seneschal harboured Tristan, Gorvenal, Kaherdin and his squire, and after Tristan bit by bit had told him the story of his life, Dinas travelled to Tintagel to learn the doings of the court. He learned that three days hence, Queen Iseult, King Mark, all their train, their equerries and their huntsmen intended leaving Tintagel for the castle at White-Lands, where the great hunts awaited them. Then Tristan gave his ring of green jasper to the seneschal and the message he was to deliver to the Queen.

DINAS

OF

LIDAN

Dinas accordingly returned to Tintagel, climbed the stair and entered the hall. Under the canopy King Mark and Iseult the Fair sat over a game of chess. Dinas seated himself on a stool beside the Queen, as though to observe her play, and twice, pretending to point out moves to her, he posed his hand on the chess board: the second time, Iseult perceived on one of his fingers the jasper ring. Great joy immediately overwhelmed her. Lightly she jarred Dinas' arm, so that several pawns fell in a heap.

"Look, seneschal," said she, "you have disturbed my game, and in a way that prevents my resuming it."

Mark left the hall, Iseult repaired to her chamber and had the seneschal called to her:

"Friend, you bear a message from Tristan?"

"Yes, Queen, he is at Lidan, hidden in my castle."

"Is it true that he has taken a wife in Brittany?"

"Queen, they have told you the truth. But he swears that he has not betrayed you; that not for a single day has he ceased cherishing you above all women; that he will die if he does not see you again, only one time: he adjures you to consent to it, by the promise you gave him the last time he spoke with you."

Iseult was silent for a while, thinking on the other Iseult. At length she answered:

"Yes, the last time he spoke with me, I said, I well remember, 'If ever I see the ring of green jasper, neither tower nor stronghold, nor royal prohibition will keep me from doing the will of my friend, be it wisdom or folly. . . .'"

"Queen, two days hence the court is to leave Tintagel for White-Lands; he instructs you that he will be concealed along the route in a thicket of thorns; he summons you to take compassion on him."

"I promised: neither tower, stronghold nor royal prohibition would keep me from doing the bidding of my friend."

The day after the morrow, while all Mark's court prepared to leave Tintagel, Tristan and Gorvenal, Kaherdin and his squire put on their helmets, took their swords and shields and by hidden ways stole towards the appointed spot. Through the forest two roads led to White-Lands: one broad and beaten, over which the cavalcade was to pass, the other rocky and neglected. Tristan and Kaherdin posted their squires on the latter: they were to await them at this spot with their horses and shields. They themselves slipped through the brush and hid in a thicket. On the road, Tristan laid a branch of hazelwood bound with a shoot of woodbine. Soon the cavalcade appeared down the road. It was led by the attendants of King Mark. In fine array there advanced the heralds and the marshals, the cooks and the cup-bearers; then came the chaplains, then the masters of the hounds with beagles and greyhounds on the leash, then the falconers bearing the birds on their left wrists, then the huntsmen, then the knights and the barons: they trotted by arranged in double file, and it was a fine sight to see them, richly mounted on horses caparisoned in velvet sewn with goldsmith-work. Then King Mark passed and Kaherdin marvelled to see his counsellors about him, two on one side, two on the other, all clad in cloth of gold or scarlet.

The cortege of the Queen now followed. At its head came the laundresses and the chamber-maids, then the wives and the daughters of the barons and the counts. These passed in single file, escorted each by a young knight. Finally there advanced a palfrey ridden by the loveliest woman Kaherdin ever had laid eyes on: she was beautifully made of body and face, with falling hips, well-defined eyebrows, laughing eyes and tiny teeth; a gown of red samite covered her; a string of gold and jewels bound her smooth brow.

"It is the Queen," whispered Kaherdin.

"The Queen?" said Tristan. "No, that is Camille, her maid."

There followed on a grey palfrey another lady, whiter than snow in February, redder than roses; her bright eyes sparkled like stars reflected in a fountain.

"Now I see her, there is the Queen!" said Kaherdin.

"Ah, no," said Tristan, "that is Brangien the Faithful."

But at once the road grew bright, as though the sun suddenly had shone out through the foliage of the great trees, and Iseult the Blonde appeared. Duke Andret, whom God damn, rode by her side.

Instantly from the thorn-copse there rose the songs of white-throats and skylarks, and Tristan put all his tenderness into these melodies. The Queen understood the signal of her friend. On the ground she perceived the branch of hazelwood about which the woodbine tightly clung, and thought in her heart: "So is it with us, friend: neither you without me nor I without you." She reined her palfrey, dismounted, went to a hackney that bore a shrine inlaid with jewels; therein on a purple carpet crouched the dog Pticru. She took it in her arms, petted it with her hand, stroked it with her ermine mantle, played happily with it. Then, having replaced it in its house, she turned towards the thorn-copse and said aloud:

"Birds of this wood, who have rejoiced me with your songs, I take you into my service. While my lord Mark rides to White-Lands I shall sojourn in my castle of St. Lubin. Birds, attend me thither: this evening I will richly recompense you as good minstrels."

Tristan heard these words and rejoiced. But Andret the felon was troubled. He helped the Queen into her saddle and the cortege drew away.

Now hear a sorry tale! While the royal cortège was passing, far off on the other road, where Gorvenal and Kaherdin's squire guarded their masters' horses, there passed an armed knight named Bleheri. From afar he recognized Gorvenal and Tristan's shield: "What do I see," thought he, "that is Gorvenal and the other is Tristan himself." He spurred his horse towards them and cried "Tristan!" But the two squires already had turned bridle and were flying. Launched in pursuit of them Bleheri repeated:

"Tristan, hold, I conjure you, by your prowess!"

But the two squires would not turn about. Then Bleheri cried:

"Tristan, hold, I conjure you in the name of Iseult the Fair!"

Thrice he conjured the fugitives in the name of Iseult the Fair. It was in vain: they disappeared, and Bleheri only captured one of their horses, which he took with him as his prize. He reached the castle of St. Lubin at the moment the Queen descended there. And, having found her alone, he said to her:

"Queen, Tristan is in this country. I saw him on the rocky road which leads from Tintagel. He took to his heels. Thrice I cried to him to stop, calling on him in the name of Iseult the Fair; but he had taken fright, he did not dare await me."

"Fair sir, what you are saying is falsehood and folly: how should Tristan be in this country? How would he have fled before you? How would he not have drawn up, conjured in my name."

"Nevertheless, Lady, I saw him, so well that I captured one of his horses. You can see it, all caparisoned, down there, in the open."

But Bleheri saw Iseult wax wroth. It pained him, for he loved Tristan and the Queen. He left her presence, sorry that he had spoken.

Then Iseult wept and said, "Unhappy woman; I have lived too long, since I have seen the day when Tristan makes game of me and reviles me! Formerly, if conjured in my name, what foe would he not have faced? He is bold of body: if he fled before Bleheri, if he did not deign to stop at the name of his friend, ah, it is because the other Iseult possesses him! Why did he return? He had betrayed me and wanted to shame me besides. Was he not satisfied by my old sorrows? Then let him return, reviled in his turn, to Iseult of the White Hands!"

She called Perinis the Faithful and told him the news which Bleheri had brought her. She added:

"Friend, find Tristan on the rocky road which leads from Tintagel to St. Lubin. Tell him that I do not salute him, and that he should not make bold to come near me, for I will have him driven off by men-at-arms and valets."

Perinis set out on the quest and at last found Tristan and Kaherdin. He gave them the Queen's message.

"Brother," cried Tristan, "what are you saying? How could I have fled before Bleheri, since as you see, we have not even our horses? Gorvenal and the squire are guarding them, we did not meet them at the trysting-place and we are still searching for them."

At this moment Gorvenal and Kaherdin's squire returned and told of what had happened.

"Perinis, fair sweet friend," Tristan said, "go back quickly to your lady. Tell her that I send her greetings and love, that I have not failed in the loyalty I owe her, that she is dearer to me than any other woman; tell her to send you back to me bearing her regards; I will wait here till you return."

Perinis accordingly went back to the Queen and repeated to her what he had seen and heard. But she did not believe him:

"Ah, Perinis, you were my counsellor and my confidant, and my father destined you for my service even as a child. But Tristan the sorcerer has won you with his lies and his gifts. You also, you have betrayed me: get you gone!"

Perinis knelt before her:

"Mistress, I hear bitter words. Never in my life have I felt greater anguish. But I do not care for myself: it is for you I sorrow, mistress, who are doing injustice to my lord Tristan, and who will regret it when it is too late."

"Get you gone, I do not believe you! You too, Perinis, Perinis the Faithful, you have betrayed me!"

Tristan waited long for Perinis to bring him the forgiveness of the Queen. Perinis did not come.

At dawn, Tristan wrapped himself in a wide ragged mantle. In spots he painted his face with vermilion and walnut-stain, to make it resemble that of a sick man ravaged by leprosy. In his hands he took a hanaper of grained wood for the collection of alms, and a leper's rattle. He entered the streets of St. Lubin and disguising his voice, begged of all passers. If only he might see the Queen!

At last she came from the castle; Brangien and her women, her valets and her men-at-arms accompanied her. She took the road to the church. The leper followed the valets, shook his rattle, begged in a miserable voice:

"Queen, be good to me; you do not know the need in which I am!"

She knew him by his fair form, by his stature. All of her trembled, but she refused to look at him. The leper implored her, and pitiful it was to hear him. He dragged himself after her:

"Queen, if I dare come close to you, be not wroth: have pity on me, for I have deserved that you have."

But the Queen called the valets and the men-at-arms:

"Drive off this leper!" she said to them.

The valets shoved and struck him. He beat them off and cried:

"Queen, have mercy!"

And Iseult laughed aloud. Her laughter rang even as she entered the church. Hearing her laugh, the leper drew away. The Queen took several steps forward in the nave of the minster; then her limbs gave way; she fell on her knees, with head to the pavement, and outstretched arms.

That very day Tristan took leave of Dinas in such downcast mood that he seemed to have lost his mind, and his ship set sail for Brittany.

Alas, before long the Queen repented. When she learned from Dinas that Tristan had left in such dejection, she began to think that Perinis had told the truth; that Tristan had not fled, when conjured in her name; that she had most unjustly driven him away. "What," thought she, "I have driven you away, Tristan, friend! Henceforth you will hate me, and never will I see you again. Never will you know of my repentance, even, nor what punishment I shall impose on myself and offer you as a small proof of my remorse!"

From that day, to punish herself for her error and her folly, Iseult the Fair put on a hairshirt and wore it against her skin.

TRISTAN

MAD

Tristan saw Brittany again, Carhaix, Duke Hoël, and his wife Iseult of the White Hands. All welcomed him, but Iseult the Fair had driven him away: nothing else mattered. Long he languished, far from her, till on a day he knew he must see her again, even if she had him basely beaten by her men-at-arms and valets. Far from her, death came surely; and he had rather die at once than day by day. Who lives in sorrow is like a man dead. And he desired some death, but that the Queen might know it was for love of her he had died; then would death come easily.

So he left Carhaix secretly, telling no man, neither his kindred nor even Kaherdin, his brother in arms. He went in rags afoot (for no one marks the beggar on the high road) till he came to the shore of the sea.

He found in a haven a great ship ready, the sail was up and the anchor-chain short at the bow.

"God save you, my lords," he said, "and send you a good journey. To what land sail you now?"

"To Tintagel," they said.

Then he cried out:

"Oh, my lords! take me with you thither!"

And he went aboard, and a fair wind filled the sail, and she ran five days and nights for Cornwall, till, on the sixth day, they dropped anchor in Tintagel Haven. The castle stood above, fenced all around. There was but the one armed gate, and two knights watched it night and day. So Tristan went ashore and sat upon the beach, and a man told him that Mark was there and had just held his court.

"But where," said he, "is Iseult, the Queen, and her fair maid, Brangien?"

"In Tintagel too," said the other, "and I saw them lately; the Queen sad, as she always is."

At the hearing of the name, Tristan suffered, and he thought that neither by guile nor courage could he see that friend, for Mark would kill him.

And he thought, "Let him kill me and let me die for her, since every day I die. But you, Iseult, even if you knew me here, would you not drive me out?" And he thought, "I will try guile. I will seem mad, but with a madness that shall be great wisdom. And many shall think me a fool that have less wit than I."

Just then a fisherman passed in a rough cloak and

cape, and Tristan seeing him, took him aside, and said:

"Friend, will you not change clothes?"

And as the fisherman found it a very good bargain, he said in answer:

"Yes, friend, gladly."

And he changed and ran off at once for fear of losing his gain. Then Tristan shaved his wonderful hair; he shaved it close to his head and left a cross all bald, and he rubbed his face with magic herbs distilled in his own country, and it changed in colour and skin so that none could know him, and he made him a club from a young tree torn from a hedge-row and hung it to his neck, and went barefoot towards the castle.

The porter made sure that he had to do with a fool and said:

"Good morrow, fool, where have you been this long while?"

And he answered:

"At the abbot of St. Michael's wedding, and he wed an abbess, large and veiled. And from the Alps to Mount St. Michael how they came, the priests and abbots, monks and regulars, all dancing on the green with croziers and with staves under the high trees' shade. But I left them all to come hither, for I serve at the King's board to-day."

Then the porter said:

"Come in, lord fool; the Hairy Urgan's son, I know, and like your father."

And when he was within the courts the serving men ran after him and cried:

"The fool! the fool!"

But he made play with them though they cast stones and struck him as they laughed, and in the midst of laughter and their cries, as the rout followed him, he came to that hall where, at the Queen's side, King Mark sat under his canopy.

And as he neared the door with his club at his neck, the King said:

"Here is a merry fellow, let him in."

And they brought him in, his club at his neck. And the King said:

"Friend, well come; what seek you here?"

Tristan replied in a strangely distorted voice:

"Sire, good and noble King among all, I knew that at the sight of you, my heart would melt in tenderness. God save you, fair King."

"Friend, what seek you in these parts?"

"Iseult," said he, "whom I love so well; I bring my sister with me, Brunehild, the beautiful. Come, take her, you are weary of the Queen. Take you my sister and give me here Iseult, and I will hold her and serve you for her love."

The King said laughing:

"Fool, if I gave you the Queen, where would you take her, pray?"

"Oh! very high," he said, "between the clouds and heaven, into a fair chamber glazed. The beams of the sun shine through it, yet the winds do not trouble it at all. There would I bear the Queen into that crystal chamber of mine all compact of roses and the morning."

The King and his barons laughed and said:

"Here is a good fool at no loss for words."

But the fool as he sat at their feet gazed at Iseult most fixedly.

"Friend," said King Mark, "what warrant have you that the Queen would heed so foul a fool as you?"

"Oh! Sire," he answered gravely, "many deeds have I done for her, and my madness is from her alone."

"What is your name?" they said, and laughed.

"Tristan," said he, "that loved the Queen so well, and still till death will love her."

But at the name the Queen angered and weakened together, and said: "Get hence for an evil fool!"

But the fool, marking her anger, went on:

"Queen Iseult, do you mind the day, when, poisoned by the Morholt's spear, I took my harp to sea and fell upon your shore? Your mother healed me with strange drugs. Have you no memory, Queen?"

But Iseult answered:

"Out, fool, out! Your folly and you have passed the bounds!"

But the fool, still playing, pushed the barons out, crying:

"Out! madmen, out! Leave me to counsel with Iseult, since I come here for the love of her!"

And as the King laughed, Iseult blushed and said:

"King, drive me forth this fool!"

But the fool still laughed and cried:

"Queen, do you mind you of the dragon I slew in your land? I hid its tongue in my hose, and, burnt of its venom, I fell by the roadside. Ah! what a knight was I then, and it was you that succoured me."

Iseult replied: "Silence! You wrong all knighthood by your words, for you are a fool from birth. Cursed by the seamen that brought you hither; rather should they have cast you into the sea!"

The fool burst out laughing.

"Queen Iseult," he still said on, "do you mind you of your haste when you would have slain me with my own sword? And of the hair of gold? And of how I stood up to the seneschal?"

"Silence!" she said, "you drunkard. You were drunk last night, and so you dreamt these dreams."

"Drunk, and still so am I," said he, "but of such a draught that never can the influence fade. Queen Iseult, do you mind you of that hot and open day on the high seas? We thirsted and we drank together from the same cup, and since that day have I been drunk with an awful wine."

When the Queen heard these words which she alone could understand, she rose and would have gone.

But the King held her by her ermine cloak, and made her to sit down again.

"Wait a while, Iseult, let us hear these ravings to the end. Fool, have you any skills?"

"I have served kings and counts."

"Honestly, do you know how to hunt with dogs, with falcons?"

"Indeed, when it pleases me to hunt in the forest, I know how to seize with my hounds the cranes which fly through the clouds; with my beagles, the swans, the white or coloured geese, the wood-doves; with my bow, the loons and bitterns."

All laughed merrily and the King asked:

"And what do you catch, brother, when you hunt big game?"

"I catch everything I find; with my traps I take timber-wolves and brown bears; with my gerfalcons, I take stags; roebucks and does with my sparrow-hawks; foxes with my pilgrim-hawks; hares with my merlins. And when I return to the house that harbours me, I know how to play the game of quarter-staves, deal out blows among the squires, tune my harp and sing pieces of music, love the queens and throw neat shavings into the brooks. In truth, am I not a good minstrel? This very day you have seen how I can spar with my stick."

He struck about him with his staff.

"Be off from here, Cornish lords," cried he. "Why do you tarry? Have you not already eaten your fill? Are you not stuffed?"

The King, having had his fun with the fool, called for his charger and his hawks and went to hunt with his knights and squires. Iseult said to him:

"Sire, I am weak and sad; let me go rest in my room; I am tired of these follies."

And she went to her room in thought and sat upon her bed, calling herself a slave and saying:

"Why was I born? Brangien, dear sister, life is so hard to me that death were better! There is a fool without, shaven criss-cross, and come in an evil hour, and he is warlock, for he knows in every part myself and my whole life; he knows what you and I and Tristan only know."

Then Brangien said: "It may be Tristan."

But—"No," said the Queen, "for he was the first of knights, but this fool is foul and made awry. May God curse him, and cursed be the hour in which he was born, and cursed the ship which brought him hither instead of sinking him out there in the depths."

"My lady!" said Brangien, "soothe you. You curse and excommunicate overmuch these days! Where indeed have you learned such ways? May be he comes from Tristan?"

"I cannot tell. I know him not. But go find him, friend, and see if you know him."

So Brangien went to the hall where the fool still sat alone. Tristan knew her and let fall his club and said:

"Brangien, dear Brangien, before God! have pity on me!"

"Foul fool," she answered, "what devil taught you my name?"

"Lady," he said, "I have known it long. By my head, that once was fair, if I am mad the blame is yours, for it was yours to watch over the wine we drank on the high seas. The cup was of silver and I held it to Iseult and she drank. Do you remember, lady?"

"No," she said, and as she trembled and left he called out: "Pity me!"

He followed and saw Iseult. He stretched out his arms, but in her shame, sweating agony she drew back, and seeing that she shunned him, Tristan trembled for shame and anger, stepped back towards the wall by the door, and said in his distorted voice:

"I have lived too long, for I have seen the day that Iseult repulses me, refuses her love, holds me in contempt. Iseult, how hard love dies! Iseult, a welling water that floods and runs large is a mighty thing; on the day that it fails it is nothing; so love that turns."

But she said: "Brother, I look at you and doubt and tremble, and I know you not for Tristan."

"Queen Iseult, I am Tristan indeed that do love you; mind you for the last time of the dwarf, and of the flour, and of the blood I shed in my leap and of the gift I sent you, the dog Pticru with the fairy bell? Do you not remember the bits of shaven wood which I cast into the brook?"

Iseult looked at him, sighed, knew not what to say or believe, saw that he knew all things, yet it would have been madness to acknowledge that he was Tristan; and Tristan said to her:

"My lady Queen, I know well you have withdrawn yourself from me and I accuse you of treason. Nevertheless I have known days, my fair one, in which you loved me well. It was in the forest depths, under the hut of branches. Do you not remember the day when I gave you my good dog Hodain? Ah, he at least has always loved me, and for my sake he would leave Iseult the Fair. Where is he? What have you done with him? He at least would recognize me."

"He recognize you? You speak madness; for since Tristan left, he has stayed below, crouched in his kennel, and bites every man who comes near him. Brangien, bring him here."

Brangien brought him.

"Come here, Hodain," said Tristan. "You were mine and I take you back."

No sooner had Hodain heard his voice than he yanked his leash out of Brangien's hands, sprang to his master, rolled at his feet, licked his hands and barked for joy.

"Hodain," cried the fool, "blessed be the pains I took in rearing you! You have bidden me better welcome than she whom I so loved. She will not recognize me: will she at least recognize this ring which she gave me, long since, with tears and kisses, on the day we parted? This little ring of jasper has never left me: often in my torment I have asked advice of it, often have I moistened its green jasper with my hot tears."

Iseult saw the ring. She opened wide her arms:

"Come! Take me, Tristan!"

Then Tristan ceased to distort his voice:

"Friend, how could you so long have failed to recognize me, longer than this very dog? What mattered this ring? Do you not feel how far sweeter it would have been to have been recognized at the very mention of our former love? What mattered the sound of my voice? You should have overheard the sound of my heart."

"Friend," said Iseult, "perhaps I did hear it sooner than you thought; but we are surrounded by treachery: should I, like this dog, have followed my wishes at the risk of having you caught and killed under my eyes? I saved you and myself. Neither the mention of your past life, nor the sound of your voice, not even this very ring, proved anything to me, for all these might have been the evil tricks of a sorcerer. Nevertheless I yield myself at the sight of this ring: did I not swear, as soon as I should see it again, at the risk of my life to always do what you bade me, be it wisdom or folly? Wisdom or folly, come; take me, Tristan!"

And her eyes darkened and she fell; but when the light returned she was held by him who kissed her eyes and her face. He drew her behind the arras. In his arms he held the Queen.

To have their fun with the fool, the valets let him sleep under the stairs to the hall, like a dog in his kennel. Patiently he endured their banter and their blows, for again and again, taking on his own form and beauty, he passed from his dirty hole to the chamber of the Queen.

So passed they three full days. But, on the third, two maids that watched them told the traitor Andret, and he put spies well-armed before the women's rooms. And when Tristan would enter they cried:

"Back, fool! Go lie on your truss of straw!"

But he brandished his club laughing, and said:

"What! May I not kiss the Queen who loves me and awaits me now?"

And they feared him for a mad fool, and he passed in through the door.

Then, being with the Queen for the last time, he held her in his arms and said:

"Friend, I must fly, for they are wondering. I must fly, and perhaps shall never see you more. My death is near, and far from you my death will come of desire."

"Oh friend," she said, "fold your arms round me close and strain me so that our hearts may break and our souls go free at last. Take me to that happy place of which you told me long ago. The fields whence none return, but where great singers sing their songs for ever. Take me now."

"I will take you to the Happy Palace of the living, Queen! The time is near. We have drunk all joy and sorrow. The time is near. When it is finished, if I call you, will you come, my friend?"

"Friend," said she, "call me and you know that I shall come."

"Friend," said he, "God send you His reward."

As he went out the spies would have held him; but he laughed aloud, and flourished his club, and cried:

"Peace, gentlemen, I go and will not stay. My lady sends me to prepare that shining house I vowed her, of crystal, and of rose shot through with morning."

And as they cursed and drave him, the fool went leaping on his way.

§

DEATH

When he was come back to Brittany, to Carhaix, it happened that Tristan, riding to the aid of Kaherdin his brother in arms, made war on a baron named Bedalis. He fell into an ambush laid by Bedalis and his brothers. Tristan slew the seven brothers. But he himself was wounded by a blow from a spear, and this spear was poisoned.

Painfully he returned to the castle of Carhaix and had his wounds dressed. Many doctors came but none could cure him of the poison, for they did not even find it. They fixed no plaster to draw the poison forth, and vainly pounded and ground their roots, culled their herbs, boiled their potions. And Tristan weakened, the poison spread throughout his body, he paled and his bones showed.

Then he knew that his life was going, and that he must die, and he had a desire to see once more Iseult the Fair, but he could not seek her, for the sea would have killed him in his weakness, and how could Iseult come to him? And sad, and suffering the poison, he awaited death.

He called Kaherdin secretly to tell him his pain, for they loved each other with a loyal love; and as he would have no one in the room save Kaherdin, nor even in the neighbouring rooms, Iseult of the White Hands began to wonder. She was afraid and wished to hear, and she came back and listened at the wall by Tristan's bed; and as she listened one of her maids kept watch for her.

Now, within, Tristan had gathered up his strength, and had half risen, leaning against the wall, and Kaherdin wept beside him. They wept their good comradeship, broken so soon, and their friendship.

"Fair friend and gentle," said Tristan, "I am in a foreign land where I have neither friend nor cousin, save you; and you alone in this place have given me comfort. My life is going, and I wish to see once more Iseult the Fair. Ah, did I but know of a messenger who would go to her! For now I know that she will come to me—Kaherdin, my brother in arms, by our friendship, by the nobility of your heart, by our comradeship, I entreat you: undertake this errand for me, and if you carry my word, I will become your liege, and I will cherish you beyond all other men."

And as Kaherdin saw Tristan broken down, his heart reproached him and he said:

"Fair comrade, do not weep; I will do what you desire, even if it were risk of death I would do it for you. Nor no distress nor anguish will let me from doing it according to my power. Give me the word you send, and I will make ready."

And Tristan answered:

"Thank you, friend; this is my prayer: take this ring, it is a sign between her and me; and when you come to her land pass yourself at court for a merchant, and show her silk and stuffs, but make so that she sees the ring, for then she will find some ruse by which to speak to you in secret. Then tell her that my heart salutes her; tell her that she alone can bring me comfort; tell her that if she does not come I shall die. Tell her to remember our past time, and our great sorrows, and all the joy there was in our loyal and tender love. And tell her to remember that draught we drank together on the high seas. For we drank our death together. Tell her to remember the oath I swore to serve a single love, for I have kept that oath."

But behind the wall, Iseult of the White Hands heard all these things; and she almost swooned. Tristan continued:

"Hasten, my friend, and come back quickly, or you will not see me again. Take forty days for your term, but come back with Iseult the Fair. And tell your sister nothing, or tell her that you seek some doctor. Take my fine ship, and two sails with you, one white, one black. And as you return, if you bring Iseult, hoist the white sail; but if you bring her not, the black. Now I have nothing more to say, but God guide you and bring you back safe."

He sighed, wept and bewailed his fate, and Kaherdin also wept, embraced Tristan and took leave.

With the first fair wind Kaherdin took the open, weighed anchor and hoisted sail, and ran with a light air and broke the seas. They bore rich merchandise with them, dyed silks of rare colours, enamel of Touraine, wines of Poitou, and gerfalcons from Spain, for by this ruse Kaherdin thought to reach Iseult. Eight days and nights they ran full sail to Cornwall.

Now a woman's wrath is a fearful thing, and all men fear it, for according to her love, so will her vengeance be; and their love and their hate come quickly, but their hate lives longer than their love; and they will make play with love, but not with hate. Standing by the wall, Iseult of the White Hands had overheard everything. How much she had loved Tristan! . . . At last she learned of his love for another. She kept every word in mind: if only some day she could, how she would avenge herself on her whom he loved most in the world. But she hid it all; and when the doors were open again she came to Tristan's bed and served him with food as a lover should, and spoke him gently and kissed him on the lips, and asked him if Kaherdin would soon return with one to cure him . . . but all day long she thought upon her vengeance.

And Kaherdin sailed and sailed till he dropped anchor in the haven in Tintagel. He landed, placed a great gerfalcon on his wrist, took with him a cloth of rare dye and a cup well chiselled and worked, and made a present of them to King Mark, and courteously begged of him his peace and safeguard that he might traffick in his land; and the King gave him his peace before all the men of his palace.

Then Kaherdin offered the Queen a buckle of fine gold; and "Queen," said he, "the gold is good."

Then taking from his finger Tristan's ring, he put it side by side with the jewel and said:

"See, O Queen, the gold of the buckle is the finer gold; yet that ring also has its worth."

When Iseult saw what ring that was, her heart trembled and her colour changed, and fearing what might next be said she drew Kaherdin apart near a window, as if to see and bargain the better; and Kaherdin said to her, low down:

"Lady, Tristan is wounded of a poisoned spear and is about to die. He sends you word that you alone can bring him comfort, and recalls to you the sorrows that you bore together. Keep you the ring—it is yours."

But Iseult answered, nearly swooning:

"Friend, I will follow you; get ready your ship tomorrow at dawn."

And on the morrow at dawn the Queen announced that she wished to hunt with falcons and had her dogs and birds made ready. But Duke Andret, ever on the watch, accompanied her. When they reached the fields not far from the shore of the sea, a pheasant whirred up. Andret unleashed a falcon to seize it; but the day was clear and fine: the falcon soared aloft and disappeared.

"See, Sir Andret," said the Queen, "the falcon has perched itself on the mast of a ship which I do not know. Whose is it?"

"Mistress," said Andret, "it is the ship of that Breton merchant who yesterday made you a present of a gold clasp. Let us go there to recapture our falcon."

Kaherdin had stretched a plank as a gangway from his ship to the shore. He came to meet the Queen:

"Lady, if it please you, enter my ship and I will show you my rich wares."

"Willingly, sir," said the Queen.

She dismounted, stepped to the plank, crossed it, and stepped into the ship. Andret sought to follow her and was on the plank when Kaherdin from the deck struck him with his oar: Andret staggered and fell into the sea. He tried to swim; Kaherdin struck him blow after blow and held him under the waves and cried:

"Die, traitor! These are your wages for the evil you have done to Tristan and to the Queen Iseult."

Thus God avenged the lovers on the felons who had so hated them. All four were dead: Guenelon, Gondoïne, Denoalen, Andret.

They raised anchor, stepped mast and hoisted sail. The fresh wind of morning whistled in the rigging and swelled the sails. Out of the harbour, towards the high seas, white and flashing under the rays of the sun, sailed the ship.

But at Carhaix Tristan lay and longed for Iseult's coming. Nothing now filled him any more, and if he lived it was only as awaiting her; and day by day he sent watchers to the shore to see if some ship came, and to learn the colour of her sail. There was no other thing left in his heart.

He had himself carried to the cliff of the Penmarks, where it overlooks the sea, and all the daylight long he gazed far off over the water.

Hear now a tale most sad and pitiful to all who love. Already was Iseult near; already the cliff of the Penmarks showed far away, and the ship ran heartily, when a storm wind rose on a sudden and grew, and struck the sail, and turned the ship all round about, and the sailors bore away, and sore against their will they ran before the wind. The wind raged and big seas ran, and the air grew thick with darkness, and the ocean itself turned dark, and the rain drove in gusts. The yard snapped, and the sheet; they struck their sail, and ran with wind and water. In an evil hour they had forgotten to haul their pinnace aboard; it leapt in their wake, and a great sea broke it away.

Then Iseult cried out: "God does not will that I should live to see him, my love, once—even one time more. God wills my drowning in this sea. Oh, Tristan, had I spoken to you but once again, it is little I should have cared for a death come afterwards. But now, my love, if I do not come to you, it is because God does not will it, and this is my deepest grief. My death is as nothing to me: since God wishes it, I accept it; but, friend, when you learn of it, you will die, well I know. Our love is such that you cannot die without me nor I without you. I see your death before me at the same time as my own. Alas, friend, I have failed of my wish: it was to die in your arms, to be buried in your tomb; but we both have failed. I shall die alone, and without you, disappear in the sea. Perhaps you will not hear of my death, you will live, ever hoping that I come. If God wishes, you may even grow well again. . . . Ah, maybe afterwards you will love another woman, you will love Iseult of the White Hands. I do not know how it will be with you: for my part, if I knew you dead, I would not live on. May God bring us together, friend, or may I heal you, or may we both die of the same wound."

And thus the Queen complained so long as the storm endured; but after five days it died down. Kaherdin hoisted the sail, the white sail, right up to the very masthead with great joy; the white sail, that Tristan might know its colour from afar: and already Kaherdin saw Brittany far off like a cloud. Hardly were these things seen and done when a calm came, and the sea lay even and untroubled. The sail bellied no longer, and the sailors held the ship now up, now down the tide, beating backwards and forwards in vain. They saw the shore afar off, but the storm had carried their boat away and they could not land. On the third night Iseult dreamt this dream: that she held in her lap a boar's head which befouled her skirts with blood; then she knew that she would never see her lover again alone.

Tristan was now too weak to keep his watch from the cliff of the Penmarks, and for many long days, within walls, far from the shore, he had mourned for Iseult because she did not come. Dolorous and alone, he mourned and sighed in restlessness: he was near death from desire.

At last the wind freshened and the white sail showed. Then it was that Iseult of the White Hands took her vengeance.

She came to where Tristan lay, and she said:

"Friend, Kaherdin is here. I have seen his ship upon the sea. She comes up hardly—yet I know her; may he bring that which shall heal thee, friend."

And Tristan trembled and said:

"Beautiful friend, you are sure that the ship is his indeed? Then tell me what is the manner of the sail?"

"I saw it plain and well. They have shaken it out and hoisted it very high, for they have little wind. For its colour, why, it is black."

And Tristan turned him to the wall, and said:

"I cannot keep this life of mine any longer." He said three times: "Iseult, my friend." And in saying it the fourth time, he died.

Then throughout the house, the knights and the comrades of Tristan wept out loud, and they took him from his bed and laid him on a rich cloth, and they covered his body with a shroud. But at sea the wind had risen; it struck the sail fair and full and drove the ship to shore, and Iseult the Fair set foot upon the land. She heard loud mourning in the streets, and the tolling of bells in the minsters and the chapel towers; she asked the people the meaning of the knell and of their tears. An old man said to her:

"Lady, we suffer a great grief. Tristan that was so loyal and so right, is dead. He was open to the poor; he ministered to the suffering. It is the chief evil that has ever fallen on this land."

But Iseult, hearing them, could not answer them a word. She went up to the palace, following the way, and her cloak was random and wild. The Bretons marvelled as she went; nor had they ever seen woman of such a beauty, and they said:

"Who is she, or whence does she come?"

Near Tristan, Iseult of the White Hands crouched, maddened at the evil she had done, and calling and lamenting over the dead man. The other Iseult came in and said to her:

"Lady, rise and let me come by him; I have more right to mourn him than have you—believe me. I loved him more."

And when she had turned to the east and prayed God, she moved the body a little and lay down by the dead man, beside her friend. She kissed his mouth and his face, and clasped him closely; and so gave up her soul, and died beside him of grief for her lover.

When King Mark heard of the death of these lovers, he crossed the sea and came into Brittany; and he had two coffins hewn, for Tristan and Iseult, one of chalcedony for Iseult, and one of beryl for Tristan. And he took their beloved bodies away with him upon his ship to Tintagel, and by a chantry to the left and right of the apse he had their tombs built round. But in one night there sprang from the tomb of Tristan a green and leafy briar, strong in its branches and in the scent of its flowers. It climbed the chantry and fell to root again by Iseult's tomb. Thrice did the peasants cut it down, but thrice it grew again as flowered and as strong. They told the marvel to King Mark, and he forbade them to cut the briar any more.

The good singers of old time, Béroul and Thomas of Built, Gilbert and Gottfried told this tale for lovers and none other, and, by my pen, they beg you for your prayers. They greet those who are cast down, and those in heart, those troubled and those filled with desire, those who are overjoyed and those disconsolate, all lovers. May all herein find strength against inconstancy, against unfairness and despite and loss and pain and all the bitterness of loving.

JOSEPH BÉDIER

(1864–1938),

the distinguished French medieval-
ist and literary historian, has made
an important contribution to our
understanding of French literary
history in general and the Middle
Ages in particular. Modern theories
of the fabliaux *and the* chansons de
geste *are based on two studies by*
him. He also produced a critical edi-
tion of the Chanson de Roland, *and*
with Paul Hazard, his pupil, he was
joint editor of the two-volume Lit-
térature Française, *one of the most*
valuable modern general histories
of French literature.